# Come Away by Yourselves

*A Guide to Prayer for Busy Catholics*

# Come Away by Yourselves

*A Guide to Prayer for Busy Catholics*

~

based on
**The Way to Converse Always and Familiarly with God**

An excellent work
of the great Doctor of the Church,
Saint Alphonsus Liguori,
from Volume II of his Ascetical Works.

by
Charles D. Fraune

Slaying Dragons Press

Nihil Obstat:     Rev. Matthew Kauth, S.T.D.
                  March 19, 2019
                  Solemnity of Saint Joseph

An original work by Charles D. Fraune, published in 2018. This Third Edition is slightly updated to include a new subtitle and cover design.

Copyright © 2024 by Slaying Dragons Press.

ISBN: 9781961721081

Quotes from Saint Alphonsus de Liguori are from Volume II of the Ascetical Works, from the section titled "The Way to Converse Always and Familiarly with God," as edited by Rev. Eugene Grimm. Scripture verses as quoted by Saint Alphonsus de Liguori are from the Douay-Rheims version of Sacred Scripture. Unless otherwise noted, all other quotes of Sacred Scripture are from the RSVCE.

The Revised Standard Version of the Bible: Catholic Edition, copyright © 1965, 1966 the Division of Christian Education of the National Council of the Churches of Christ in the United States of America. Used by permission. All rights reserved.

Cover art: James Tissot, *Jesus Commands the Apostles to Rest*, Brooklyn Museum, public domain. Cover updated by Caroline Green.

www.SlayingDragonsPress.com
2024

*To the glory of the Most Holy Trinity,
in gratitude to Saint Alphonsus Maria de Liguori
for his example, wisdom, holiness,
and intercession.*

# Table of Contents

# Note on the Third Edition

This new edition is practically identical to the original *Come Away By Yourselves*. The primary difference is the subtitle. As the book became more widely read, it was realized that it would be better to describe the book less narrowly in the subtitle. The book is intended to aid busy Catholics in their effort to achieve times of fruitful prayer. The original subtitle was "a guide to making a retreat," which reflected an earlier project known as *The Retreat Box*. This project preceded the emergence of *Slaying Dragons Press*. Thus, the language in the book pivots around the concept of making a "retreat." In this edition, this language is left intact. As a result, while one reader can easily utilize the book as an aid to making a retreat in the form of a true "get away," at the same time, a different reader can use the book as an aid to prayer within a busy life.

In addition to the change in the subtitle, the layout of the book has been slightly modified. As a result, the page numbers will be different from the previous edition. Further, the cover design has been updated and the publisher name is now *Slaying Dragons Press*, reflecting the growth of the apostolate that began as *The Retreat Box*.

# PREFACE

This book is comprised of two sections: the first is designed as a practical guide to making a retreat; the second is a series of nine reflections, with challenges and considerations following each reflection.

Section One provides a thorough reflection on the concept of making a retreat and will help the retreatant prepare properly for a retreat. It will also help them anticipate the many challenges that will arise in the effort to set aside time, and be properly disposed, for a retreat. Our Lord calls us to a deep life of prayer and union with Him. For most people, life is incredibly busy, and time is limited, but prayer is still mandatory for peace and union with God. This section will provide a good foundation of understanding regarding the how-to of a retreat, and also provide insight into how to enter into a "retreat mode" more easily, frequently, and fruitfully, all the while within a busy life.

Section Two provides nine reflections which can be utilized at the pace with which the reader is most comfortable. Each reflection contains a list of practical suggestions at the end, based on the reflection, meant to create opportunities to put into practice what was pondered in the reflection.

# INTRODUCTION

*Come Away by Yourselves* is broken up into different Reflections, which can either be read all in one sitting, scattered throughout the day, or read daily over the course of many days, a week, or longer. It may be enjoyed by itself, or part of a package called a "Retreat Box," which we offer on our website. That Retreat Box is designed to create a spiritual retreat out of a quiet seclusion for a varying amount of time, depending on your circumstances, with coffee/tea, sacred music, some snacks, a classic spiritual book by Saint Alphonsus Liguori,[1] and a Guided Retreat based on the book.

This Retreat is designed for laymen in all states of life. Our Lord calls all men and women to a deep and intimate knowledge of Himself. This applies to the over-busy mother of many, to the stressed and time-crunched father of a family, and to the college graduate establishing himself in a career and readying himself for family life. Some will only have a few hours on a Saturday morning, some will be able to set aside a whole day, and others will be able to set aside about fifteen minutes a day for several weeks. Each approach can be made to bear fruit.

For those able to take a full day to retreat, the reflections can be read throughout the day at intervals. For those with a few hours in the morning to retreat, these can be read in one sitting, or throughout the following week(s).

After each Reflection, there are Challenges and Practical Suggestions offered to ensure that the retreatant is able to retain the insights gained during that time of reflection and meditation. There is also space provided for the retreatant to make notes.

---

1 "The Way to Converse Always and Familiarly with God"

This Notes section, at the end of each Reflection, is provided to encourage the retreatant to do a number of things. As you retreat and pray and consider the ideas, accept some of the Challenges, and put into practice some of the Suggestions, and you will have new insights into your spiritual life. In this section, simply jot them down so you do not forget, or use the whole space like a journal to elaborate on the insights gained. You may also write down the prayers that you were inspired to offer to Our Lord as a result of your reflections. This will be useful for several reasons: 1) as a reminder of the mode of prayer you were in during your retreat, 2) as a reminder of the spiritual needs you had during this time, 3) as evidence, when looking back, of God's interaction with you, and of how He answered your prayers, and 4) as a future reminder of the power of a retreat.

# Section One

~~~

# A Practical Guide to Making a Retreat

# How To Make A Retreat Within a Busy Life

*And He said to them, "Come away by yourselves to a lonely place, and rest a while."*[1]

## Principles

All Christians are called by Our Lord to come away with Him for a while. For a priest, or a monk, or a nun, this is easier – as their lives are ordered in such a way as to accommodate this and, responding to Our Lord's unique call, they chose these lives in order to secure the freedom to do this.

For laymen, living in the world, ever busy, ever complicated, and ever unstable, making a retreat on a regular basis, or ever, is often merely a dream. Sadly, when it becomes a mere dream for us, that dream often evaporates and vanishes, as do dreams each morning once we awake. The Retreat we are proposing is not one that needs to be canceled due to the busy-ness of life; it is one that can happen within that commotion.

The idea of a retreat must not be allowed to evaporate! Remember, a retreat is a dedicated time with Our Lord – this must always be in the forefront of a Christian's mind: "my God and my All!" What better way to express our belief in that phrase than by making a retreat, by giving God our scattered moments – by giving Him all that we have.

Here, again, we come back to that word: retreat. Laymen are not ordained or religious and, though we are consecrated for God by our Baptism, we do not live lives set apart only for the Lord. While we are set apart for Him, others depend on us, and are entrusted to us, and require much of our

---

1 Mark 6:30

5

available time. Thus, we must fight, in a sense, to make time to pray.

Let us name those things which necessarily consume our time: children, jobs, second jobs, household chores, paying bills, shopping, etc. One thing is important to do: remind ourselves that these are good things. Knowing that they take some of our time every day, we must also remember that these are part of life and willed by God; they are inescapable. They must not be completely blamed for our inability to pray, but must be converted into moments of prayer. Children must be loved, but clever scheduling and planning can free up some extra time. Jobs are necessary, but working toward a job with a more ideal schedule may free up some extra time. Chores and bills are necessary, but getting organized can also free up some extra time.

Make it a priority to carve out time with Our Lord, and you will find the motivation to simplify and organize, just enough, in order to find some extra time to spend alone with Him. The more we pray, the more we will be drawn to pray, and the more time will we find to do it. For laymen, making a retreat helps train us to pray constantly throughout our daily activities. Being in a constant mode of prayer is what we may expect of priests, but even they must get away often to make retreats, in order to keep up this state of prayer. How much more, then, does the laymen need to retreat, whose activities often do not revolve around spiritual things.

Here we come to an important point: the retreat for a layman is slightly mystical by nature – it must call upon a special grace from God. This is so because this retreat often must happen unplanned, or spontaneously; it often must be very brief: a dive into spiritual intimacy in five minutes. What I mean is: the best way for a layman to retreat, when he has no time to go away on a formal retreat, is to "sneak away." Consider that this is what Our Lord had to do for Himself and His Apostles.

Let's look at the Gospel of St. Mark:

> The apostles returned to Jesus, and told him
> all that they had done and taught. And he said
> to them, "Come away by yourselves to a lonely
> place, and rest a while." For many were
> coming and going, and they had no leisure
> even to eat. And they went away in the boat to
> a lonely place by themselves. Now many saw
> them going, and knew them, and they ran
> there on foot from all the towns, and got there
> ahead of them. As he landed he saw a great
> throng, and he had compassion on them,
> because they were like sheep without a
> shepherd; and he began to teach them many
> things. And when it grew late, his disciples
> came to him and said, "This is a lonely place,
> and the hour is now late; send them away, to
> go into the country and villages round about
> and buy themselves something to eat." But he
> answered them, "You give them something to
> eat."[2]

Notice what happened. They were all tired, and their
energies spent, and in need of some quiet time together with
the Lord. However, the demands of their vocation
interrupted them. The only time they had in quiet with Our
Lord was on the boat ride headed to their retreat. When they
arrived at their "lonely place," the people were waiting for
them, needy and seeking them.

Two responses are given by Our Lord when His retreat
is quickly ended. First, accepting the situation, "he had
compassion on them" and "he began to teach them many
things." Second, He empowered His Apostles, who were
themselves interrupted by their "children" when they had

---

2 Mark 6:30-37

sought a retreat, enabling them to perform a miracle, with Him, and feed five thousand people.

These two responses teach us that we must constantly seek to get away to a lonely place to rest awhile with Our Lord, and that we must also be ready for that quiet time to be interrupted. Further, it teaches us that, despite the brevity of the retreat, and the suddenness of the interruption, Our Lord will be with us in that moment, and will remain with us after the retreat, to such an extent that He can perform miracles for us within our vocation.

This gives an answer to why we need to retreat. It shows that these times of retreat, even very brief ones, are still times of true intimacy with the all-powerful and all-loving Lord. This same Lord is outside of time, and can work within our lives in ways that we cannot even imagine.

If we sneak away with Him often, He can then calm the storms in our hearts, and thus in our homes. He can help us with the chaos of a busy home filled with children. He can teach us how to rest with Him and drop our excessive worries. He can help us to see that we impose on ourselves too many unnecessary burdens, which can be put down. He can help us to see that, despite our tight budgets, it is still possible to give to others with great generosity. Our Lord, who will not be outdone in generosity, will reward our efforts, and bless His beloved children.

### Practical Considerations

*This section is directed toward those who are setting aside about an hour or more for a retreat, though those who can only do "sneak away" retreats may still find this helpful.*

In the next section, we will focus on the best way to utilize the time you are able to set aside. Then, we will give some guidance specifically tailored to the different retreat approaches listed.

One motto to keep in mind while considering the following items is "Know thyself."

## Time of day:

The best time of day to make a retreat will depend on you. Consider the following questions. Are you a morning person? An evening person? A night owl? When is your mind the sharpest? The dullest? When are you most reflective? When is your house the quietest? The noisiest?

Usually, there is one time of day when you feel more mentally awake and when your mind is the sharpest. Perhaps it is while waking up with a cup of coffee. Perhaps it is while slowing down in the evening with a cup of tea. Perhaps it is late at night, or early in the morning, when all else in the world is sleeping. A time that is quiet is key, though. However, in addition to the quiet, you need to be alert. This calls to mind another consideration: sleep.

## Sleep:

You might think that a good night's rest is best before an important time of prayer. However, that might not be the case. Consider it this way: if you regularly get less sleep than you would like, due to children or the demands of life, then you are trained to live off of less sleep than is ideal. If this applies to you, what happens when you set aside a morning to "sleep in"? Some people feel groggy the next day! While this might be good for your health, it might not be good for prayer.

For people who live by coffee, they are used to thinking in the context of a storm of fatigue and caffeine. They are trained for this. So, to disrupt this with an abundance of sleep might cause a disruption in your normal mental patterns and strength. Consider this before you decide to "sleep in" and make your retreat in the morning. Do what is best to achieve a prayerful disposition.

## Coffee...or tea:

Speaking of coffee, this one is a little less difficult to consider. If you are a coffee drinker, then you will want to have some good coffee ready for your retreat. If you are not a regular coffee drinker, then...well...you make the call. Know what effect coffee has on you and then decide. If it makes you jittery and nervous, you should probably skip it. If it perks you up and is a special treat, then bring it along.

One thing to consider if you enjoy coffee – perhaps don't fast from it on your retreat. You may want to fast, or be simple, or penitential, on your retreat, but, if you drink coffee daily, don't skip it on the retreat. However, you make the call. Make the choice that will best dispose you, physically and intellectually, to praying and listening. One last note, if you like coffee a lot, don't overdo it on the retreat. You will have that temptation to have another cup...and another cup...and...*jitters*.

## Sacred space:

The environment you pick for your retreat can have a strong impact on the depth of your prayer. Consider what best disposes you to reflection and act accordingly. If you are more contemplative outdoors, then go sit outdoors. If you think it might be too cold, then bundle up. The presence of a coat or a blanket can have a good psychological effect – it may help you feel comforted and secure.

Picture a monk with his hood pulled up, and his head barely visible, buried in the deep hood, alone with God as he prays in secret. You could pull the blanket over your head like that, and hide with Him in this temporary cave. Use your imagination to enter into a comfortable state for prayer. Our Lord spoke about prayer in a similar manner: But when you pray, go into your room and shut the door and pray to your

Father who is in secret; and your Father who sees in secret will reward you.[3]

You may prefer to be indoors. If so, consider the spaces in your house and how familiar they are, or what activities typically take place in them. Think ahead of time as to whether you will be distracted in a certain room. Find a space that will be the least distracting, and will not constantly draw you back to your everyday concerns. Maybe even a closet, or a laundry room, or a garage…or someone else's house, or a park…

**Distractions:**

This is a confusing consideration. Some of us may think we need absolute silence in order to focus. Some of us may be parents and no longer familiar with the sound of silence. White noise can be a great way to strike a balance. White noise is like silence in that it is the absence of fluctuating sounds. If your room is completely quiet, you may become distracted by the sound of your finger on the paper, or your chair when you shift, or by every creak of the house and chirp of a bird. If you have good white noise going, those little sounds just blend in.

It may seem a bit nitpicky, but some people can be very distracted when they are trying to find a quiet moment. So, turn on a fan, even in a bathroom, or find some subtle noise that can run in the background. Know thyself, and then decide how much noise is ideal, and how much silence is ideal. On a formal retreat at an isolated monastery, you will have less trouble finding true silence. There, the silence is powerful. Here, the silence is often interrupted, so plan accordingly.

---

3 Matthew 6:6

**Food, snacks, and fasting:**

This is another important aspect which ultimately depends on the motto: Know thyself. What happens to you when you fast? Do you get tired? Cranky? Hungry? Weak? If your stomach rumbles constantly when you fast, will that be distracting when you are trying to pray in silence? If you get sleepy when you fast, will you pass right out as soon as you sit down to pray? If you get weak when you fast, what impact does that have on your ability to think clearly and deeply?

If you like to snack while on retreat, does the enjoyment of the food become a distraction? Do these draw you back to a consideration of earthly things? Are you so sleep deprived that it is better if you graze than if you sit down for full meals? If so, then snacking is probably going to give you energy during your prayer. Are you unable to control yourself when you snack? Then, perhaps, don't snack.

You want your mind to be sharp, and your body to be awake, when you pray. So, figure out which approach to food provides the best form of focus during the limited amount of time you have for prayer. Lent is one thing – fast! – but critical and desperate getaways are another thing. Be well disposed.

Perhaps, you could fast the day before you intend to pray. You may have some insights throughout that day and will then be ready to ponder them on your retreat...with some snacks.

**Sacred music:**

Sacred music, whether hymns or Gregorian chant or polyphony, is truly inspired by the Spirit of Christ. Music is essential to the higher forms of worship, as we see in Solemn High Masses, which fill the liturgy with the most beautiful music. Sacred music and chant will truly help dispose you to prayer. Your use of traditional sacred music will depend on your level of familiarity with it.

If you are not very familiar with it, it might be good to listen to some music the day before you make your retreat, however short that retreat will be. This will simply expose you to the sounds, and to the spiritual senses that the music awakens. You may find, for example, that the third track on the CD you purchased or borrowed from a friend speaks to your soul in a way that the others do not. If so, consider beginning your retreat with that hymn. You could also decide to begin the retreat in silence and prayer, while reading the reflections in the Guided Retreat. You may then, a few minutes into your retreat, decide that that is the best time to reflect with the hymn.

If you are very familiar with sacred music, you can do this, or you may want to avoid using any music at all, since life these days is so often flooded with music and other noises. This approach is just as valid. It may be that the use of music, during the moments set aside for the retreat, amounts to lost time that could have been better used speaking to Our Lord, or reflecting on an insight, or writing in your journal.

**Technology**

Laptops, fancy phones, and music devices: these are all quite handy, fascinating, helpful, full of resources and accessibilities. They are also inseparably sources of communication, distraction, and procrastination. So, limit your reliance upon these during your retreat. Perhaps a CD player, that only plays CDs, and doesn't connect to the internet, would be best for the use of music on the retreat. Instead of bringing your phone, perhaps just wear a watch, so you know what time it is.

You need the freedom to confront your conscience, where Our Lord is trying to speak to you. It may be the case that you admit to something awkward or uncomfortable with Our Lord. If it is easy to distract yourself with something "important" on your phone, you will likely do so at that moment, and miss the opportunity to reach a new depth in your prayer. Spiritual insights await you every time you pray – be focused and open.

## Retreat Options

*The following are some considerations for each of the standard options for making a retreat.*

### Retreat Option: Full Day

If you can get away for a full day, do it. Ask people to help. Swap responsibilities with your spouse. Trade Saturdays – one goes this Saturday, the other goes the next Saturday. Perhaps end that day with a special family meal or outing or picnic in order to bring everyone back together and give the other spouse a break. There really are ways for very busy people to get away for a whole day. There are typically some quiet places to find in your area: a park, your parish, a public school track, a car ride alone, a hiking trail, a biking trail, even your own backyard.

If you are able to get away for a full day, be sure you are ready to "let go" of the day as well. Consecrate the day to Our Lord and go – but let Him take over the way the day will unfold. Have your core plan for prayer, reflections, snacks, walks and sitting, but let Him make adjustments as He sees fit. He knows what you need to think about more than you do.

### Retreat Option: One Morning…or evening

This is a classic retreat style for a layman. Saturday mornings seem to be the ideal mornings, though your "Saturday" might be a different day, if you have a unique job. On the real Saturday, the typical work week has ended, for most, and a day of flexibility has dawned. Most people are more relaxed, or have simply delayed their work until later in the day.

Consider getting up early, making some coffee, sitting on the porch or at the dining room table, looking out the window. Start praying and then read the first reflection. Sip your coffee, look out the window, think about the insights you may have had, or what the reflection led you to consider. Note anything important, or write a prayer in the notes section. If you have any consoling insights or are led to pray, do that, and with no time table.

If you only read one reflection in two hours of resting with Our Lord, because of all the thoughts it stirred, and the prayers it prompted, and the reforms it suggested, so be it. Save the rest for the next Saturday, or the next morning.

If you are an evening person, you can follow the same routine. Sometimes evenings are busier and you may be more tired, so plan accordingly. If you consider swapping the coffee for alcohol in the evening, Know thyself. Sometimes alcohol can make you sleepy, drowsy, or unable to think clearly at the end of a long and tiring day. However, sometimes a single drink can help you relax and unwind and focus. So, Know thyself.

# Fundamental Retreat Concepts

Don't be stubborn about your expectations. Let Our Lord decide what insights are best for you to receive at this time.

Tell the Lord why you think you really need what you sense you really need.

Make a humble and trustful prayer asking Our Lord to make this a fruitful retreat.

Know that the fruit of your retreat may not be borne in the time you are actually on retreat. It may show up later in the day, the next day, or the next week. The fruit may appear without you even realizing it. It might actually be better to expect it not to come while on retreat. However, one way to show your trust in Our Lord's goodness is to have in your heart a true expectation that He will act in your life in some way.

Have a clear intention on your heart when you pray. You are seeking Christ. This will become the lens through which you view and read the reflections. Seek him. Be forgetful of yourself in those moments. He will later help you understand yourself better if that is what you need.

Be excited about your retreat, from the moment you decide to do it.

Don't try to control the retreat too much. Have a rhythm you want to follow but be willing to drop it at the first prompting from Our Lord to go in a different direction.

Be ready and willing to put everything down, look off into the distance or out the window, and just think.

Beseech Our Lord to put a thought into your mind, something He wants you to know or understand, or to shine a fresh light on a truth about Him and salvation.

# What Steals Our Time

As you prepare, name those things that you allow to steal your time:

> TV, routinely watched videos and shows, video games, constantly checking the news, cleaning unnecessarily, going out to restaurants, unconstructive__ daydreaming, stewing over old wounds and current worries ...

_____

_____

_____

_____

_____

_____

_____

_____

_____

_____

_____

# Section Two

~~~

# The "Sneak-Away" Retreat

# The "Sneak-Away" Retreat

*The Retreat for busy Christians who wish to remain always with Our Lord.*

The idea of the "Sneak-Away" Retreat is at the heart of this book, as the reader will see. This is a retreat style unlike the ones mentioned earlier, and the one that most people need to master because it is actually quite accessible if we have the insight to find the time. It is something that we can do with much more frequency and flexibility. Truly, this is something that springs from the sanctified heart of the Christian, where Our Lord calls us, in His time, to come and speak to Him. It helps form a conditioned mindset, and a willingness of the heart, to attend to the One who holds the place of primacy in our lives.

Many Christians in this modern culture, particularly those in the married state, feel like they can never get a break and can never take a moment to breathe. This world is very burdensome and time consuming and distracting. Our own flaws don't help this much either. What little time there is we can figure out how to squander away. The toys this culture has offered us are very enticing, and truly very helpful with organizing and communication and entertainment. However, they also absorb our time in the process. They are shiny and fascinating, but they are not the reason we exist. We exist to come to know God, to come to love Him, and to serve Him that we may come to Heaven when our life closes.

When we clearly realize the latter truth, the busy nature of our lives can really start to feel like chaos that needs to be calmed. But, how to calm it? How to prioritize it? How to spiritually capitalize on those quiet moments of time that appear for a minute and then pass away? If you could gather them all together, you might have a decent chunk of restful quiet time; but, that's not the reality.

Here, we get to an important point: reality. We must always live in reality, not constantly in a fantasy, wishing our lives were this or that way. Life is as it is at the moment. You can work to change your life for the better, but you have to acknowledge the way it is now. If you want to start seizing your free moments for retreats and for prayer, it would be very beneficial to step back and review your routine. See where time is wasted, perhaps through human weakness or through unnecessary use of technology, or various other distractions. Tell Our Lord that you want to give Him more time, even if it is only those moments in the day when you can sneak away.

Perhaps you don't step away because the chaos of the day won't let you rest, even when you have the time. When this happens, the quiet moments are really wasted on earthly things and earthly concerns. Perhaps it is finally nap time for the kids, but it came at the end of screaming and diaper madness. Now that the kids are down, all you want to do is sit down and stare off into space, or lie down also, or just cry at the craziness of it all. This is life for a lot of Christians today. Jobs are not easy to come by, often don't pay enough, and often require both spouses to work. Parents are pressured on all sides, worried about income, kids' friends and activities, school, forming them in the Faith, finding time to spend as a family, and avoiding the pollution of the culture, among others.

This is where we must remind ourselves that we are Christians! Sometimes, and this is a shameful admission that we must make – we forget this fact. We become motivated by worldly concerns. We become servants of the culture. We become indistinguishable from non-Christians due to the amount of stress we succumb to. All of this is very difficult to resist in this generation. However, it can be done. We can live first as Christians, then as citizens of this world. If we do that, we will see where there is time to pray.

In order to make this point more solemnly from a Christian perspective, let us return to the Gospel passage quoted earlier.

> The apostles returned to Jesus, and told him all that they had done and taught. And he said to them, "Come away by yourselves to a lonely place, and rest a while." For many were coming and going, and they had no leisure even to eat. And they went away in the boat to a lonely place by themselves. Now many saw them going, and knew them, and they ran there on foot from all the towns, and got there ahead of them. As he landed he saw a great throng, and he had compassion on them, because they were like sheep without a shepherd; and he began to teach them many things. And when it grew late, his disciples came to him and said, "This is a lonely place, and the hour is now late; send them away, to go into the country and villages round about and buy themselves something to eat." But he answered them, "You give them something to eat."[1]

Before we re-analyze that passage, let us look at another, and very similar, passage:

> And when he got into the boat, his disciples followed him. And behold, there arose a great storm on the sea, so that the boat was being swamped by the waves; but he was asleep. And they went and woke him, saying, "Save, Lord; we are perishing." And he said to them, "Why

---

1 Mark 6:30-37

are you afraid, O men of little faith?" Then he rose and rebuked the winds and the sea; and there was a great calm. And the men marveled, saying, "What sort of man is this, that even winds and sea obey him?"[2]

Could you not look at your vocation as this boat in the latter story? When the stresses of this world begin to overwhelm you, remember these stories. Our Lord rebuked the Apostles for lacking faith. This means that He knew about the storm, even while He slept. When they woke Him, and they were panicking, He saw that as a lack of faith in Him. Still, He immediately rebuked the winds and the sea, and brought a great calm. It was so powerful that the Apostles marveled at His abilities to help them.

In the former story, Our Lord saw that the Apostles were tired, weary, hungry, and needing a reprieve. So, He called them away from the chaos and stress of their vocation, but had only a few minutes of peace together before they were interrupted by the people who needed their help. But, see the power of that time stolen away with Our Lord! After landing on the shore, Our Lord performed, with and through the Apostles, a tremendous miracle for their children.

### Treasured Moments of Grace
*How to Retreat in a Sneak Away moment*

So, these sneak away retreats can be the treasured moments of grace, when we pull away for a moment to rest with Our Lord. There, we will truly find refreshment. It is in these moments that we must reflect with faith, and deeply, on the images of His love that Our Lord has given to His Church.

Imagine the scene on the boat, when the Apostles were going away with Our Lord to a lonely place. We know, from

---

2 Matthew 8:23-27

other places in the Scriptures, how close the Beloved Disciple, St. John, was to Our Lord. Truly, he is the model disciple, so let us take him as our model for these sneak away retreats.

Do you recall how he is depicted at the Last Supper?

> When Jesus had thus spoken, he was troubled in spirit, and testified, "Truly, truly, I say to you, one of you will betray me." The disciples looked at one another, uncertain of whom he spoke. One of his disciples, whom Jesus loved, was lying close to the breast of Jesus; so Simon Peter beckoned to him and said, "Tell us who it is of whom he speaks." So lying thus, close to the breast of Jesus, he said to him, "Lord, who is it?" Jesus answered, "It is he to whom I shall give this morsel when I have dipped it."[3]

It is this disciple who shows no hesitation to ask Our Lord the question that is on every other Apostle's mind. Even before Our Lord announced this betrayal, St. John was lying close to the breast of Jesus. It is this disciple who loves and believes. We see this later, when it is shown that he is the only Apostle to stay with Our Lord even to the Cross.

While we do not have Our Lord physically present in the same way that St. John did, we can use our real communion with Him, and our imagination, to be close with Our Lord in a similar way. When you sneak away to be with Him, during a moment when all is calm, or when your spouse can watch the kids alone, find a comfortable place and close your eyes. You are truly in Our Lord's presence when you pray, even more so when you are in a state of grace. Do something as simple as lean up against the wall, resting your head there. Imagine that this is as close to Our Lord as you can be, and let this touch convey to your soul that you are truly

---

3 John 13:21-26

spiritually leaning up against Him, and that He is truly that close to you. Then, just sigh and say, "O, Lord."[4]

This sneak away retreat can be accomplished in a single minute. You could excuse yourself to wash your hands before a meal. Then, when you are away, alone, do as mentioned above. Let this be your monastic cell, your consecrated space, your little Heaven, your mystical moment, your secret room where the Lord and you may speak together as intimate friends. If you become accustomed to this, you can stretch the time, and take this book with you. In your secret room, read over one reflection. Perhaps you can only read a single reflection in pieces throughout the day. So be it. Every little step you take toward God is a step toward God.

Know also that these steps are sacrifices pleasing to God. Think about it: you have no time, but what little time you have, you are offering to God in order to grow in love for Him. Let this call to mind something Our Lord told His Apostles:

> And he sat down opposite the treasury, and watched the multitude putting money into the treasury. Many rich people put in large sums. And a poor widow came, and put in two copper coins, which make a penny. And he called his disciples to him, and said to them, "Truly, I say to you, this poor widow has put in more than all those who are contributing to the treasury. For they all contributed out of their abundance; but she out of her poverty has put in everything she had, her whole living."[5]

---

4 Also, "My God and my All," "My Jesus, mercy," "Come, Holy Spirit," "Behold, O Lord, Thy servant and thy son," "O Lord, I believe, help my unbelief," "O Lord, have mercy on me, a poor sinner," etc.

5 Mark 12:41-44

How sweet it must be for Our Lord to hear the voices of those children of His who have sacrificed much of the little time they have in order to spend it with Him!

See, too, the personality of Our Lord as this story reveals it. He sat down and watched everyone as they put their money in the treasury. He saw each one of them, and knew their intentions, and the amount they gave. See His delight, also, when he notices the widow, who gave to God all that she had. Imagine Him looking at you when you are stepping away to pray to Him for a few minutes. Imagine His delight! With that in mind consider the many other things He has told us.

When you sneak away, do so with confidence. Imagine that you just heard Our Lord say the following:

> "Ask, and it will be given you; seek, and you will find; knock, and it will be opened to you. For every one who asks receives, and he who seeks finds, and to him who knocks it will be opened. Or what man of you, if his son asks him for bread, will give him a stone? Or if he asks for a fish, will give him a serpent? If you then, who are evil, know how to give good gifts to your children, how much more will your Father who is in heaven give good things to those who ask him!"[6]

When you take your few minutes to pray, let these words stir confidence in you. Ask Him for what you need. Remember your primary call to holiness, and then your vocational call, and then your practical needs, and then your good desires, when you ask Him. He has promised that the Father will give good things to those who ask him! So, ask Him.

Further, Our Lord has said, "If a man loves me, he will keep my word, and my Father will love him, and we will come

---

6 Matthew 7:7-11

to him and make our home with him."[7] When you pray, you express your love for Our Lord. Be sure you are faithful to Him as well, so make repentance a key part of your prayer. For if you keep His word, He will come and make His home with you. He also said, "But when you pray, go into your room and shut the door and pray to your Father who is in secret; and your Father who sees in secret will reward you."[8]

This inner room is your soul, where you speak heart to heart with God. It is secret, and the Father will speak to you in secret. Sneak away. Be quiet; pray and listen. Remember the great calm that He brought to the sea in order to aid the Apostles. Remember also what He said to the Samaritan woman, to whom He promised to give living water: "But whoever drinks of the water that I shall give him will never thirst; the water that I shall give him will become in him a spring of water welling up to eternal life."[9] Know that this is what resides in your soul and, when you pray, pray with this knowledge. Let this living water stir within you, and let this image comfort you and further dispose you to trust and surrender to Our Lord in that moment.

## Speaking to Our Lord
*What to say to Our Lord on a Sneak-Away Retreat*

As the idea conveys, time is of the essence here. Therefore, cut right to the heart of the matter – literally. Do not focus on rote prayers first. Instead, close your eyes and tell Our Lord your deepest spiritual yearning. Be blunt, be direct, be clear. "O Lord, I long for You. Let me be satisfied with You alone!" Do this in a spirit of calm trust. When you step into that momentary solitude, know that He has drawn you there, that He is right there before you, and within you. Bury your head in your hands, or fold your hands together at

---

7 John 14:23
8 Matthew 6:6
9 John 4:14

your chest, to "hide" with Him, and enter into the monastic cell of your heart. Then, speak to the heart of the matter, that deep or secret or central craving for peace or stability or holiness or wisdom. Rest in confidence that He hears you and desires to answer you. Repeat this to Him. Establish this petition as the central theme of this critical conversation.

After this momentary retreat, look back, throughout the day, to this secret moment you spent with Our Lord. Repeat the same petition often, and with the same deep confidence. Listen, and you may hear His same voice again, assuring you that He loves you and desires to give you all that is good. Persist, then, throughout the day, in reflecting, and quickly and silently returning, to that prayer. Our Lord goes with you wherever you go. Acknowledge Him, and repeat your love and petition to Him.

# Section Three

~~~

## Reflections

# Prayers Before Each Reflection

Our Father, Who art in heaven,
Hallowed be Thy Name.
Thy Kingdom come.
Thy Will be done, on earth as it is in Heaven.
Give us this day our daily bread,
and forgive us our trespasses,
as we forgive those who trespass against us,
and lead us not into temptation,
but deliver us from evil. Amen.

Hail Mary, full of Grace, the Lord is with thee. Blessed art
thou among women, and blessed is the fruit of thy womb,
Jesus.
Holy Mary, Mother of God, pray for us sinners now, and at
the hour of our death. Amen.

Glory be to the Father, and to the Son, and to the Holy
Spirit, as it was in the beginning, is now, and ever shall be,
world without end. Amen.

Direct, we beseech Thee, O Lord, all our actions by Thy
holy inspirations, and carry them on by Thy gracious
assistance, that every prayer and work of ours may begin
always with Thee, and through Thee be happily ended,
through Christ our Lord. Amen.

O Lord, grant me an increase in Thy grace, and a new
insight into Thy love for me. Amen.

## First Reflection

# Peace is found in being able to speak to God with ease and confidence

*Prayers: Our Father, Hail Mary, Glory be, Direct we beseech Thee, O Lord grant me...page 31.*

Truly, the foundation of peace is to be able to speak to God with confidence, knowing that your manner of speaking to Him is actually pleasing to Him: a manner which is humble, sincere, acceptable, fruitful, filial.

Saint Alphonsus Liguori concludes his treatise on prayer[1] with the following paragraph:

> St. Teresa says that holy souls in this world have to conform themselves by love to what the souls of the blessed do in heaven. As the saints in heaven occupy themselves only with God, and have no other thought or joy than in his glory and in his love, so also must this be the case with you. While you are in this world, let God be your only happiness, the only object of your affections, the only end of all your actions and desires, until you come to that eternal kingdom where your love will be in all things perfected and completed, and your desires will be perfectly fulfilled and satisfied.

From this paragraph, let us remember at least two elements: the Saints in Heaven are occupied solely with God,

---

1 The classic work, "The Way to Converse Always and Familiarly with God."

and in this life, holy souls must conform themselves by love, to what the Saints do in Heaven. This love guides our actions, and becomes the purpose of our actions. Thus, our lives should be filled with acts of love of God.

This, as you note, while being a most wonderful goal, and truly what the heart should desire, can appear to be unreasonable, unaccomplishable, to most people.

Read the above paragraph once more.

Do you believe in Heaven? Do you believe that the Saints are in Heaven, beholding God face to face? It is not these teachings which typically present the problem, but the means of accomplishing the stated goal of occupying yourself with God alone.

In this quiet, and perhaps quite rare, moment of reflection, you do consciously desire a calmer and more spiritually ordered life, free of the distractions and burdens of this world. However, this is not what we must desire, for the burdens of this world will remain so long as we are in it and so long as the world continues. What we must desire is to "conform ourselves by love" to what the Saints are doing in Heaven.

In this world, we do not visibly, not intellectually, see God completely. Thus, it is by acts of devotion that we purify and solidify our love of God, providing for our souls the security we will need to stand before Him on the Day of Judgment.

*By acts of love.* How do I secure my soul in God by acts of love when life is so distracting? Know, dear soul, that the common distractions of life are willed by God, and can be converted to Him. Indeed, though, some distractions are self-imposed, and are often not necessary in our lives, and are within our power to eradicate. Others, though, more common to man's life, are unavoidable. If you are not called to flee from the distractions of the world completely, by entering into the religious life, then you are called to be holy in the midst of them. Truly, even in the religious life, as St. Therese of Lisieux taught, the distractions of this world are present and can be sanctified. What became known as her "little way" is the way of sanctifying all of the common tasks, burdens, and annoyances of life as offerings to God, thus sanctifying everything that you do. Do all things with virtue, knowing that God has willed those tasks for you at that moment, and you will grow in His grace, in His love, and in virtue. It would be as if Mary converted Martha, but Martha had to remain at her tasks. Thus Martha is a contemplative in action, so to speak.

Acts of love of God will condition your soul to pray, by demonstrating, to God and to yourself, that you actually do love Him, not simply in words but in deeds. *"My little children, let us not love in word, nor in tongue, but in deed, and in truth."*[2] For those who love do not simply say it, but they seek to demonstrate it through acts. Our Lord says, *"If you love Me, you will keep My commandments"*[3] – that is, if you love Him, you will do things which reveal this love, such as obey Him, and return the love to Him that He gave to you.

~~~~~~~

## Considerations and Challenges

Consider your typical routine. Are there a few minutes you can carve out in order to sit down with Our Lord for just five minutes? Consider whether you are more alert and insightful in the morning or in the evening, at the start of the day or at its close. If you are not already setting aside this time, consider this approach. If it is the start of the day, then set your alarm for ten minutes earlier than usual and establish five of those minutes as a time to sit down and pray. In time, add more than just five or ten minutes.

---

2 1 John 3:18
3 John 14:15

When are you most alert and reflective? Perhaps it is with your coffee, or just after a shower, or at some quiet point in your morning routine.

Throughout the day, when you have a transition between tasks, you could pause and simply call Our Lord to mind and think about Him. Then, simply offer a prayer, even a sigh, from the heart. This will have ripple effects throughout the day, and when you have time for more formal prayer.

Prayer responds to conditioning. The more you turn to Him, the more you will be turned toward Him, and the easier it will be to pray.

Consider, now, what acts of love of God you do in your average day. Are these acts frequent? Are these acts of love done willingly and lovingly, or are they done as a necessary burden, required as part of a good spiritual life?

Consider further: are there things in your day which are obstacles to performing these acts more frequently and more heartfeltly? Reflect over the day and see where some good quality time is wasted on unnecessary tasks. This time could be converted to a time of prayer.

Are there clear moments in your day where you could add more acts of love of God, or sanctify common tasks and make them into acts of love? Reflect over your day. There are many common tasks we perform, like washing dishes, sorting laundry, cleaning counters or a mirror, etc. While these require our time, they do not demand all of our focus. Thus, our minds can truly be occupied with thoughts of God while these chores are addressed. Perhaps you could transform the task into a symbol of the action of grace on your soul, which washes away filth, enables the intellect to see more clearly, and makes you an instrument of God's love in the lives of others.

**Challenges:**

Set your alarm for ten minutes early, or fifteen minutes if you know you will hit "snooze" at least once. Get up, and pick a moment in your morning routine to use those ten minutes to pray. Pick the time when you are most alert.

Find a transitional moment in your day, such as returning from lunch. Sit down at your desk (or while still standing), make the Sign of the Cross, and say a short prayer. Let it begin with a sigh, and end with an act of trust in God's providence.

Pick a common task you perform every day and speak to Our Lord while doing it.

Make a few deliberate acts of love of God[4] at set moments in your day. Pick a few concrete moments, and concrete acts of love, and do it.

Purge wasted time from your routine. Think – what is one of those wasted moments? Instead of wasting time with that task, stand up, go to a window, and pray.

Think about your life. Are there things that are obstacles to your prayer and making acts of love? Be humble, and remove them. Go to Confession if that is the solution for these issues.

---

4 O my God, I love Thee above all things, with my whole heart and soul, because Thou art all-good and worthy of all my love. I love my neighbor as myself for the love of Thee. I forgive all who have injured me, and ask pardon of all whom I have injured.

For more ideas about how to speak to Him, remember to read "The Way to Converse Always and Familiarly with God," by Saint Alphonsus.

# Second Reflection

## Our Lord is the Friend who never leaves your side, and thinks of you at every moment

*Prayers: Our Father, Hail Mary, Glory be, Direct we beseech Thee, O Lord grant me... page 31.*

Let us now speak of one of the motivations for turning all things into an offering of love for God. Let us turn again to Saint Alphonsus:

> Friends in the world have some hours in which they converse together, and others during which they are apart; but between God and you, if you wish, there shall never be one hour of separation: *Thou shalt rest, and thy sleep shall be sweet: the Lord will be at thy side.*[1] You may sleep, and God will place himself at your side, and watch with you continually: *I will repose myself with Him, and He shall be a comfort in my cares and grief.*[2] When you take your rest, he departs not from beside your pillow; he remains thinking always of you, that when you wake in the night he may speak to you by his inspirations, and receive from you some act of love, of oblation, of thanksgiving; so as to keep up even in those hours his gracious and sweet converse with you. Sometimes also he will

---

[1] "Quiesces, et suavis erit somnus tuus. . . . Dominus enim erit in latere tuo." Prov. iii. 24.

[2] "Conquiescam cum ilia . . . et erit allocutio cogitationis." Wis. viii. 9-16,

speak to you in your sleep, and cause you to hear his voice, that on waking you may put in practice what he has spoken: *I will speak to him in a dream.*[3]

He is there also in the morning, to hear from you some word of affection, of confidence; to be the depositary of your first thoughts, and of all the actions which you promise to perform that day to please him; of all the griefs, too, which you offer to endure willingly for his glory and love. But as he fails not to present himself to you at the moment of your waking, fail not you, on your part, to give him immediately a look of love, and to rejoice when your God announces to you the glad tidings that he is not far from you, as once he was by reason of your sins; but that he loves you, and would be beloved by you: and at that same moment he gives you the gracious precept, *Thou shalt love the Lord thy God with thy whole heart.*[4]

See here, as the Saints do, the friendship of God for His adopted children! As Our Lord has said, *"I will not now call you servants: for the servant knoweth not what his lord doth. But I have called you friends: because all things whatsoever I have heard of my Father, I have made known to you."*[5] Affectionate, too, is Our Lord for us, as Saint Alphonsus describes. He has all eternity to spend with you, for He is not bound by time and space – thus, you are truly the only care He has, and He can completely give you His attention, distracted by no other concern, for He has none. He has constructed the universe for you, and was not tired after doing so. His labors are made

---

[3] "Per somnium loquar ad ilium." Num. xii. 6.
[4] "Diliges Dominum Deum tuum ex corde tuo." Deut. vi. 5.
[5] John 15:15 DR

easy for they are motivated by love, and by a love more powerful and sincere than we could ever imagine.

Picture, as Saint Alphonsus describes, Our Lord sleeping next to you, never taking His eyes off of you, whispering to you while you sleep, ready for you to wake that He might converse with you. The monastic tradition of vigil prayer makes sense when you think of Our Lord in this way. Monks will rise in the middle of the night to go and pray to the Lord. Imagine the pleasure and the joy this gives Our Lord, that His children would rise to pray to Him, and at a time when they are so burdened with drowsiness. What rewards must He have prepared for those who make such a sacrifice of love!

~~~~~~~

### Considerations and Challenges

When you first awake in the morning, think about how you tend to greet the new day. It is a gift from God. Do you greet it with a groan or a sigh? Are you passively ready, annoyed, angry, or just plain tired? Often, the way we awake can set the tone for the day.

Take some time to admire creation. This is the first revelation God gave us. Creation reveals God's glory. It is the art of the Divine Artist. There are many lessons embedded within it. See that the Lord, your dear Friend, is the One who made it for you.

Set your alarm for 1:00 am. When it goes off, turn off the alarm and simply say, "Hello, my Lord." - or - When you awake at 1:00am, rise then, without hitting snooze, and go to a spot in your house where you have an Image of Our Lord. Go to that Image, kneel, make the Sign of the Cross, and simply greet Our Lord. Briefly thank Him for everything. Ask Him to help you to be good and to love Him as He deserves to be loved. Slowly recite the Our Father. Conclude with a prayer from the heart, even if it amounts to, "O Lord, I love You, and I am so tired. Thank you for helping me rise from sleep, to greet You, my Redeemer, but I must again return there. I will see you when I rise. Amen."

Place an image of Our Lord next to your bed. Glance at it before you turn off the lights. As you close your eyes and fall asleep, think of Him.

A sample prayer: "Thank you, my Lord, for making me, that I might share your eternal glory. Thank you for all the gifts you offer to me. Help me to see them as Your gifts, which You desire will incline me to Your friendship. I love you, Lord. Grant me the grace to remain close to You always."

# Third Reflection

## Make yourself ready for Our Lord, who is ever ready for you

*Prayers: Our Father, Hail Mary, Glory be, Direct we beseech Thee, O Lord grant me... page 31.*

Your retreat is hopefully making you think more frequently, or more deeply, about your spiritual life at this point. Be sure, as you set aside time to reflect, that you are quieting all the noises that compete for your attention. The Lord speaks, but He is often drowned out by the busyness of the world, and of your own distracted mind. *"And he that received the seed among thorns, is he that heareth the word, and the care of this world and the deceitfulness of riches choketh up the word, and he becometh fruitless."*[1]

One way to remedy this is to journal. Perhaps, at this point, as the Holy Spirit has stirred your attention more, you are noticing more clearly those things in your heart that are obstacles to focusing on Our Lord more completely. Consider, now, writing down your concerns. Often, when we first go to prayer, and we quiet our thoughts so as to hear the Lord speaking, we start remembering all the things we have to do that day, and all that troubles us. This voice of remembering can often be quite loud and demanding, as if now, in this silence, you are being required to solve all of your problems and worries. But, you say, "I am here trying to pray – Lord, help me!" This is good and right, but do not become agitated, or you will become even more distracted.

---

[1] Matthew 13:22 DR

Tell yourself that these are valid concerns and dilemmas, and write them down in the journal so you are assured that you won't forget them. You can then revisit the journal after prayer and begin addressing the concerns of the day. If a new thought enters your mind while you are trying to pray, and it begins to distract you from speaking and listening to Our Lord, write it down – then return peacefully to the Lord. Eventually, your mind will calm and you will be able to shift from cares of the world to the concerns of the Lord.

An important truth is relevant here, which Saint Alphonsus addresses: God waits for us. He waits for us to tell Him our concerns and needs. He waits and is ready to answer, for He knows what we will say. He knows the inner workings of our soul better than we do, and He knows what we need better than we do. Hence, when He does not answer a prayer as we had hoped, it is because He knows what we need better than we do.

Imagine a man who thinks the pain in his foot is merely a bruise from hitting a rock when he slipped on a hike. He takes care to loosen his shoes and keeps an eye on the bruise, and expects it to go away in a few days. On the fourth day, it is just as sore as on the first. Then, he decides to submit his injury to a doctor. The doctor then informs him that a bone in his foot is broken, and a different treatment is necessary. This treatment restores the man's health, but it only came through the doctor, who knew the true source of the pain.

Likewise, when our lives are disordered and chaotic and without peace, we must first present these problems to the Lord and ask that He heal them. Then, we must resign ourselves to His will and to His way of healing them. There, we will find peace.

To do this, we must have confidence in Our Lord and in His desire to hear us. The wisdom of Saint Alphonsus is indispensable:

> Never, then, forget his sweet presence, as do
> the greater part of men. Speak to him as often

as you can; for he does not grow weary of this nor disdain it, as do the lords of the earth. If you love him, you will not be at a loss what to say to him. Tell him all that occurs to you about yourself and your affairs, as you would tell it to a dear friend. Look not upon him as a haughty sovereign, who will only converse with the great, and on great matters. He, our God, delights to abase himself to converse with us, loves to have us communicate to him our smallest, our most daily concerns. He loves you as much, and has as much care for you, as if he had none others to think of but yourself. He is as entirely devoted to your interests as though the only end of his providence were to succor you, of his almighty power to aid you, of his mercy and goodness to take pity on you, to do you good, and gain by the delicate touches of his kindness your confidence and love. Manifest, then, to him freely all your state of mind, and pray to him to guide you to accomplish perfectly his holy will. And let all your desires and plans be simply bent to discover his good pleasure, and do what is agreeable to his divine heart: *Commit thy way to the Lord:*[2] *and desire of Him to direct thy ways, and that all thy counsels may abide in Him.*[3]

Say not, But where is the need of disclosing to God all my wants, if he already sees and knows them better than I? True, he knows them; but God makes as if he knew not the necessities about which you do not speak to him, and for which you seek not his aid. Our

---

[2] "Revela Domino viam tuam." Ps. xxxvi. 5.

[3] "Et pete ab eo ut vias tuas dirigat et omnia consilia tua in ipso permaneant." Tob. iv. 20.

Saviour knew well that Lazarus was dead, and yet he made as if he knew it not, until the Magdalene had told him of it, and then he comforted her by raising her brother to life again.

Our Lord is a King, but a King who is eternal, and who thus can receive all of His subjects at the same time. There is no need to wait in line to petition Him for some favor or blessing. The excuse, in order to delay praying, that you do not wish to bother Him is completely unfounded! He is the King of your heart, and there He sits, waiting for His one subject to approach Him. All of His decrees, all of His providence, all of the protections, all of His benevolence, is dedicated to you – and this from a King who is God Himself, the conqueror of all your enemies, the supplier of all your needs, the food for which you hunger. He longs to rescue you, to feed you, to nurture you, to have you reign with Him, as His friend and companion for all eternity.

~~~~~~~

### Considerations and Challenges

As you note the distractions that bombard your mind, and the other tasks that fill your day, be honest with your spiritual situation. When, during your day, do you place these earthly concerns over your friendship with Our Lord? Are there times when you know you were simply worrying about your earthly concerns, instead of actually carrying them out? That time of worrying is wasted time. Instead of worrying, at that moment pray. Pray knowing that what Saint Alphonsus just said is true. Then, approach your task with a sense of freedom, knowing that Our Lord will guide you as you live out your day and approach the trials and frustrations that may come. If you submit your work to Him in this manner, He will enlighten you as to the best course to take. Remember, your work, and His goal, is to ensure that you safely navigate this earthly pilgrimage without taking your eyes and your heart off of the Lord.

The more effort you exert to quiet your mind of concerns and fears and troubles, the calmer your mind will generally tend to be, and the easier it will be to pray.

Take a day and silence all television, computer, and radio noises. Do this at home, at work and while driving. The silence will seep into your soul and mind. You will process your thoughts and concerns more promptly when they arise, and when you stop to pray, you will be able to focus more. If the silence becomes awkward, take some time to read Scripture or journal, which will help occupy your thoughts with holy ideas.

Set some mandatory prayer benchmarks for the day. Be prudent about that. If you need to start with "I will pray the Our Father, the Hail Mary, and the Glory Be once today" then start with that. Give God a priority place in the day, even if it is just for a minute or two. An example of a goal could be to pray for **at least** fifteen minutes a day.

If the journal space in this book is not sufficient, don't hesitate – go and buy a journal. Carefully pick one that is comfortable for you to write in.

When you pray, and you present your requests to Our Lord, stop and let Him direct the conversation at that point. Let Him lead.

Ignore any negative voices that say, "Don't waste God's time. He already knows what you need." Tell Him.

Engage your imagination while you pray. Imagine the all-powerful One sitting on a throne in your heart. Imagine Him either in a state of glory or crowned with thorns. If you need Him to be the One who can empathize with your troubles, imagine Him crowned with thorns. Then, instead of complaining, turn away from yourself, and stir up pity for Our Lord, pierced with so many thorns. Console Him with your love and fidelity. If the glory of Our Lord is more appealing at the moment, imagine Him enthroned in your heart, radiating life and grace, as the conqueror of sin and death, the Victor over evil, who is actively and continuously drawing you into this victory with Him. Let His glory scatter your fears, reminding you that if you hold fast to Him, you will enter into endless peace.

# Fourth Reflection

## Our Lord cares for even your trivial concerns

*Prayers: Our Father, Hail Mary, Glory be, Direct we beseech Thee, O Lord grant me... page 31.*

A man, who admittedly did not pray much, once said that he thought God was not concerned about the petty things in our lives and that we need not bother Him with those. However, this could not be farther from the truth! Our Lord wants to hear even the smallest of our concerns.

Do you ever speak to Our Lord about trivial matters? Do you ever ask him for some favor that seems of no consequence, but which would be pleasing to you? Perhaps a breeze when you are outdoors, or a little more snow before the storm passes, or just one more shooting star when gazing at the heavens? These are not too troublesome for the Almighty! One devout soul remarked that he, finding great joy in snowfall, found himself to be disappointed when a winter storm did not live up to the forecast, and the snow turned to sleet and freezing rain. Finding himself lacking in the consolation he found in the mystery and beauty of snow, which blankets the world in calm and purity, he asked Our Lord to make it snow heavily, such that he would not be able to see even ten feet in front of him. That prayer was heard, and in the morning the storm shifted, bringing four inches of snow in two hours, falling so heavily that the man could not see more than twenty feet in front of him.

Is this man foolish to pester Our Lord solely that the world may be blanketed in calm and purity? By no means! For such a one, his desire to see the world calm and pure reflects his longing to be likewise, that God may grant, in His generosity, such a gift to him, to be pure and to be at peace. *"Blessed are the pure in heart, for they shall see God."* [1] It is God who bestows this gift of purity on those who ask Him. *"If you then being evil, know how to give good gifts to your children: how much more will your Father who is in heaven, give good things to them that ask him?"* [2]

Reflect here on how Our Lord has taken care of you in some trivial matter...

_____

_____

_____

_____

_____

_____

_____

Further, does God will that we make such a use of creatures in our effort to come closer to Him? Let us hear what Saint Alphonsus says:

> He will not be displeased that in your desolations you should go to your friends to find some relief; but he wills you chiefly to have recourse to himself. At all events, therefore, after you have applied to creatures, and they have been unable to comfort your heart, have recourse to your Creator, and say

---

[1] Matthew 5:8
[2] Matthew 7:11

to him, Lord, men have only words for me; *my friends are full of words;*[3] they cannot comfort me, nor do I any more desire to be comforted by them; Thou art all my hope, all my love.

Are not the friends he mentions creatures, and, in a sense, the creatures also friends? *"The heavens shew forth the glory of God, and the firmament declareth the work of his hands."*[4] Therefore, it is not wrong to turn to created things for comfort, such as the coffee or tea or chocolate that keeps you awake and focused when you are tired, or the chair with the nice cushion which makes sitting not so tiresome. Though in excess these could be indulgent and sinful, when used as a means to come closer to Our Lord, they are true "friends," in the sense that they point you toward God. So long as the reason for using created things, or for praying for created comforts, is that it would aid your leisure and your search for deeper union with God, Our Lord is inclined to answer.

With this as your inclination, you will begin to see that all things in life can be used to turn your heart and intellect to the truths of Faith and serve as reminders of God's presence with you. Let us hear Saint Alphonsus as he speaks eloquently on this matter:

> Then, that you may be able to keep yourself ever in a state of recollection and union with God, as long as you live, and as far as may be possible, turn everything that you may see or hear into an occasion for raising your mind to God, or for taking a glance at eternity. For example, when you see running water, reflect that your life is also in like manner running on, and carrying you nearer and nearer to death. When you see a lamp going out for want of oil, reflect that thus also one day you will have to

---

[3] "Verbosi amici mei." Job, xvi. 21.
[4] Psalm 18:1 DR [RSVCE=19:1]

bring your life to its end. ...When you behold the sea in a calm or a storm, consider the difference that there is between a soul when in the grace, and when out of the grace, of God. When you see a tree that is withered, consider that a soul without God is serviceable for nothing but to be cast into fire... When it thunders, and you become alarmed, reflect how those miserable ones who are damned tremble as they hear continually in hell the thunders of the divine wrath...

When your eye rests on scenes in the country or along the shore, on flowers or fruits, and you are delighted by the sight and scent of all, say, Behold, how many are the beautiful creatures that God has created for me in this world, in order that I may love him; and what further enjoyments does he not keep prepared for me in Paradise? St. Teresa used to say that when she saw any beautiful hills or slopes, they seemed to reproach her for her own ingratitude to God. And the Abbot de Ranee, founder of La Trappe, said that the beautiful creatures around him reminded him of his own obligation to love God. St. Augustine also said the same, crying out aloud, *"Heaven, and earth, and all things tell me to love Thee."*[5] It is related of a certain holy man, that in passing through the fields he would strike with a little stick the flowers and plants which he found, saying, "Be silent; do not reproach me any longer for my ingratitude to God. I have understood you; be silent; say no more." When St. Mary Magdalene of Pazzi held in her hand any beautiful fruit or flower, she used to

---

[5] "Coelum et terra, et omnia quae in eis sunt, mihi dicunt ut amem te." Conf. 1. 10, c. 6

feel herself smitten by it with divine love, saying to herself, "Behold, my God has thought from eternity of creating this fruit, this flower, in order to give it me as a token of the love which he bears towards me."

When you see rivers or brooks, reflect that as the water which you behold keeps running on to the ocean without ever stopping, so ought you to be ever hasting on to God, who is your only good. When you hear the birds sing, say, Hearken, O my soul, to the praise which these little creatures are giving to their Creator; and what are you doing? Then do you also praise him with acts of love. On the other hand, when you hear the cock crow, recall to your memory that there once was a time when you also, like Peter, denied your God; and renew your contrition and your tears. So, likewise, when you see the house or place where you have sinned, turn yourself to God, and say, *"The sins of my youth and my ignorance remember not, O Lord."*[6]

When you behold any valleys, consider that as their fertility is owing to the waters that run down from the mountains, so from heaven do graces descend upon the souls of the humble, and pass by the proud. When you see a beautifully ornamented church, consider the beauty of a soul in a state of grace, which is a real temple of God. When you behold the sea, consider the immensity and the greatness of God. When you see fire, or candles lighted on an altar, say, How many years is it since I ought to have been cast into hell to burn? But since Thou, O Lord, hast not sent me there, make this heart of mine burn with love for

---

[6] "Delicta juventutis mese, et ignorantias meas, ne memineris." Ps. xxiv. 7.

Thee, as that wood or those candles burn. When you look up at the sky, all studded with stars, say with St. Andrew of Avellino, "O my feet, you will one day have those stars beneath you." Then, in order frequently to recall to mind the mysteries of our Saviour's love, when you see hay, a manger, or caves, let the Infant Jesus in the stable of Bethlehem be present to your recollection. When you see a saw, a hammer, a plane, or an axe, remember how Jesus worked like a mere lad, in the shop at Nazareth. Then if you see ropes, thorns, nails, or pieces of wood, reflect on the Passion and Death of our Redeemer. St Francis of Assisi, on seeing a lamb, would begin to weep, saying, "My Lord like a lamb was led to death for me." Again: when you see altars, chalices, or patens, recall to mind the greatness of the love which Jesus Christ has borne us in giving us the Most Holy Sacrament of the Eucharist.

Many are the examples that Saint Alphonsus has given of created realities which secretly speak a language which the devout soul can understand!

Make note, dear retreatant, of those images which stood out to you. Was it the statement by St. Andrew of Avellino, who said, gazing upon the beauty of the stars, that one day those stars would serve as the foundation for his feet, as he walks in Heaven with God? Was it the love that filled the heart of St. Mary Magdalene of Pazzi when she realized that the Lord created every delightful fruit on the earth in order to communicate to her the depth of His love? Was it the thought that, as Our Lord bestows such wondrous gifts to all men on the earth, how much more glorious must be those gifts which He holds ready for those who come to Him in Heaven? Or was it the parallel between a beautiful church and a soul in the state of grace?

Perhaps these reflections led to your own images, to things of this world that speak of those spiritual realities which are most important to you. Modern examples, which Saint Alphonsus would likely have never seen, can also be mentioned. One that comes to mind is a simple light switch. In turning the lights off in a room, it can remind us of the swiftness with which death might greet us, and how we must be prepared. In turning the lights on in a room, it can be as the moment when a soul emerges into heavenly glory, and the darkness of this world passes away. Another that comes to mind is the beauty and brilliance of a house well-decorated for Christmas, with garland and wreaths and ribbons and lights, shining and stunning in the midst of the dark night. Such, too, will be the bodies of the Blessed, when they shine forever in Heaven after rising from the dead.

These images can deeply stir the spirit and the intellect. Let them…and let Our Lord, through them, stir your soul with a renewed longing for holiness.

~~~~~~~

## Considerations and Challenges

Look at the created world differently, and see how all things point to God and to your effort to come closer to him. Note a few of these in your journal, and tell Our Lord how you wish to achieve that purity and dignity and holiness which you see mirrored in these created realities.

Ask Our Lord for something trivial, not to put Him to the test, but simply to speak lovingly to Him as your Lord and Creator, always accepting His will in the end.

Think about your friendships, "creature comforts," and foods that you turn to in order to boost your mood. How good and beneficial are these friendships? Do they make you think of

God, or do they bind you to the worries of this passing world? Are the friendships superficial, or do they raise you from burdensome worries and encourage you on the path of virtue?

Take a moment, the next time you crave a yummy snack, and take that snack with you to a quiet place. Sit down, start praying and thinking with God. Take your journal. Snack with God for a while.

Go for a walk outside, or sit on the porch when you have some time. Take note of the elements of creation that are present. Just observe. Then take note of the elements of creation that are enjoyable to you. Reflect on the enjoyment. Then connect that to the fact that God made them just for you. Do birds sound pleasant? Say, "I give You praise, O Lord!" Is there a squirrel scurrying funnily? Thank God.

Next time, when you eat a peach or an apple or something straight from a tree or a vine or a bush, pause first and say, "This was once just dirt." Then…remark on how people seldom see these fruits as living miracles, proofs of God's existence.

# Fifth Reflection

## On the ease with which we may approach Our Lord in prayer

*Prayers: Our Father, Hail Mary, Glory be, Direct we beseech Thee, O Lord grant me... page 31.*

Consider the first words, and the opening lines, of Saint Alphonsus on the matter of conversing with God.

> HOLY Job was struck with wonder to consider our God so devoted in benefiting man, and showing the chief care of his heart to be, to love man and to make himself beloved by him.

Job, who is revered by the Church as a Saint, and is treated as such by Saint Alphonsus, exclaims to the Lord, reflecting the above understanding, *"Why dost Thou set Thy heart upon him [man]?"* The Lord *sets His heart* upon us. The Lord, who created the universe and all things within it, and who brought us into being from nothing, and will take us to Himself at the end of time; this same Lord *sets His heart upon* us. The living Heart of God, revealed through the Incarnation of Our Lord Jesus Christ, is *set upon* man.

This requires thoughtful reflection.

Imagine when the heavens and the earth were brought forth in six days by the Almighty. This work of His hand was crafted in order to be a gift to one in whom He delights: man. All things are made for man. Even the Angels, who are more glorious than man, were created not for themselves but to serve man and the order of creation. Man is the only creature whom God made for its own sake, who is oriented toward God alone, and created solely to seek and find God. Man is made to live with God. God is the only end, the only purpose for man's life. All other created things exist for man's benefit. This demonstrates that the Heart of the Living God is set upon man; the Living God made all things to serve man's needs, for man is the ultimate reason for His work of creation.

And there is still more. Hear Our Lord state the full purpose of His Incarnation, and the powerful image of fire which Sacred Scripture uses: *I came to cast fire upon the earth; and would that it were already kindled!*[1] This fire is not just for punishment when He comes as Judge, but can also be seen to point to His mercy and charity.[2] *For God sent not his Son into the world, to judge the world, but that the world may be saved by him.*[3] Recall the image of the Sacred Heart of Jesus, which Our Lord also revealed to His Church: a Heart inflamed with divine love:

> "Behold this Heart, Which has loved men so much, that It has spared nothing, even to exhausting and consuming Itself."[4]

The Letter to the Hebrews references this fire of God, stating that *our God is a consuming fire.*[5] The very next verse states, *Let fraternal charity abide in you.*[6] Thus, God is a fire, burning with divine Charity, so intense that God chooses to become a man, and go courageously into the pit of death itself, in order to rescue His lost but beloved children.

So far we have seen that Our Lord has *set His Heart upon us*, He has brought all created things into being for our good,

---

[1] Luke 12:49
[2] caritas, i.e. divine love
[3] John 3:17 DR
[4] part of the revelation of the Sacred Heart to St. Margaret Mary
[5] Hebrews 12:29
[6] Hebrews 13:1

and His Heart is *burning with Charity* for man. As you reflect on the truth that you may approach Our Lord with familiarity and affection, remember that He said:

> I will not now call you servants: for the servant knoweth not what his lord doth. But I have called you friends: because all things whatsoever I have heard of my Father, I have made known to you.[7]

Further, St. Paul states that Our Lord is *the firstborn among many brethren*[8] and St. Matthew depicts Our Lord thus:

> And stretching forth his hand towards his disciples, he said: Behold my mother and my brethren. For whosoever shall do the will of my Father, that is in heaven, he is my brother, and sister, and mother.[9]

What does this all reveal but that Our Lord, through grace, is drawing us into a relationship with Him that is familial – not just familiar, but in His family! So long as we are doing the will of the Father, we are in His family. But we are not merely "in His house," for he states, *If any one love me, he will keep my word, and my Father will love him, and we will come to him, and will make our abode with him.*[10] The one who does the will of the Father will have Him as the guest in his own soul.

From an earlier reflection, we saw that Saint Alphonsus depicted Our Lord even resting on the pillow next to you, watching you while you sleep, waiting for you to stir, that He might speak to you. As the Divine Guest in your soul, it is as if your heart is the pillow on which He reclines, and by which

---

[7] John 15: 15 DR
[8] Romans 8:29 DR
[9] Matthew 12: 49-50 DR
[10] John 14:23 DR

He may easily speak to you and you to Him. Remember how the beloved disciple would recline against the Heart of the Savior – the Savior longs for this love from His children, and will return this love in like manner. This deep love for Our Lord is what He desires from us. Let us imitate the beloved disciple and cultivate this level of intimacy and trust.

Let's take a brief look at the scene in which St. John is depicted leaning against Our Lord's chest:

> When Jesus had said these things, he was troubled in spirit; and he testified, and said: Amen, amen I say to you, one of you shall betray me. The disciples therefore looked one upon another, doubting of whom he spoke. Now there was leaning on Jesus' bosom one of his disciples, whom Jesus loved. Simon Peter therefore beckoned to him, and said to him: Who is it of whom he speaketh? He therefore, leaning on the breast of Jesus, saith to him: Lord, who is it? Jesus answered: He it is to whom I shall reach bread dipped. And when he had dipped the bread, he gave it to Judas Iscariot, the son of Simon.[11]

What does this scene reveal? It reveals that the one who leans against the Heart of Christ has no fear or hesitation to speak to Him, but an ease and love in doing so. The voice of the trusting and familial disciple is loved and immediately received by Our Lord, who gives him the answer which all the disciples are seeking to know. Notice, too, that St. Peter, who stands away from Our Lord in the scene, is not comfortable asking Our Lord this most necessary question.

So, what does this mean? It means that the one who dwells ever with the Lord loves to speak with Him, and knows how to speak with Him, and Our Lord, who rests with the disciple, does not hesitate to respond. So, you must rest

---

[11] John 13: 21-26 DR

in the Lord, as your beloved Friend and Teacher – rest next
to Him, and allow Him to rest with you. Then, speak freely
to Him – tell him everything, and ask Him every burdensome
question.

Saint Alphonsus says:

> If it be a great mistake, as has been already
> said, to converse mistrustfully with God, – to
> be always coming before him as a slave, full of
> fear and confusion, comes before his prince,
> trembling with dread, – it would be a greater
> to think that conversing with God is but
> weariness and bitterness. No, it is not so: *Her
> conversation hath no bitterness, nor her company
> any tediousness.*[12] Ask those souls who love him
> with a true love, and they will tell you that in
> the sorrows of their life they find no greater,
> no truer relief, than in a loving converse with
> God.
>
> Now this does not require that you
> continually apply your mind to it, so as to
> forget all your employments and recreations.
> It only requires of you, without putting these
> aside, to act towards God as you act on
> occasion towards those who love you and
> whom you love.
>
> Your God is ever near you, nay, within
> you: *In Him we live, and move, and be.*[13] There is
> no barrier at the door against any who desire
> to speak with him; nay, God delights that you
> should treat with him confidently. Treat with
> him of your business, your plans, your griefs,
> your fears, – of all that concerns you. Above

---

[12] "Non enim habet amaritudinem conversatio illius, nec taedium convictus illius."
Wis. viii. 16.
[13] "In ipso enim vivimus, et movemur, et sumus." Acts, xvii. 28.

all, do so (as I have said) with confidence, with
open heart. For God is not wont to speak to
the soul that speaks not to him; forasmuch as,
if it be not used to converse with him, it would
little understand his voice when he spoke to it.

If you have ever felt intimidated by God, or by the idea
of speaking to Him, of approaching Him, and of
understanding how to ask the Him for a favor, let that
dissipate. Let it now be that you are not intimidated but
shocked, shocked by, and grateful for, the intensity of His
love for us! That He would call us *friends* and also treat us as
such. Let us turn to Him, and embrace the beauty and power
of His love, and say "yes" and "let it be done," as did Our Lady.

If He wishes you to pray to Him constantly, and to be
always with Him, yet you find it difficult, do you not think
He will supply the grace and means to do it? If He loves us
so, and is truly God, He will not hesitate even for a second to
take you by the hand and unto Himself. Remember how Our
Lord treated St. Peter, when He granted him the power to
walk on water:

> But seeing the wind strong, he was afraid: and
> when he began to sink, he cried out, saying:
> Lord, save me. And immediately Jesus
> stretching forth his hand took hold of him, and
> said to him: O thou of little faith, why didst
> thou doubt?[14]

Our Lord *immediately* took hold of St. Peter, and asked
him why he doubted. All you must do is sincerely extend your
hand: an open hand, an unfettered hand, a trusting hand, a
desiring hand, a hand ready to hold the Hand of its Savior.

Let us conclude with two statements from Saint Alphonsus:

---

[14] Matthew 14:30-31 DR

He disdains not, but delights that you should use towards him that confidence, that freedom and tenderness, which children use towards their mothers.

Consider, you have no friend nor brother, nor father nor mother, nor spouse nor lover, who loves you more than your God.

~~~~~~~

## Considerations and Challenges

Knowing these things, ask Our Lord to free you that you may love Him and spend time with Him. Tell Him that you wish to spend more time with Him, on a regular basis, but you do not know how to carve out that time. Tell Him you know that He can arrange your life so that you have that time, and that He can call to you when those times appear, that you may see them and seize them for prayer. Make this prayer with confidence. Especially if you yourself do not perceive any sort of available time in your day, make this prayer with confidence and give the Lord the opportunity to show you how much He really loves you. Simply be ready for Him to work, and be willing to let Him do so.

Set an alarm or reminder on your phone, so it repeats daily, at a good moment, with the message, "What is Our Lord thinking about right now?" The answer is not trite or sappy, but true: You.

Read about and practice the *Sneak Away Retreat* approach.

Make a list with the following categories: business/job, plans for future (near and far), griefs and sorrows, fears and worries, family concerns. Then, pray to Our Lord and tell Him about all of these areas of your life. When you are finished, say, "I trust in Your providence, O Lord. Help me to accept all things as coming from or permitted by You. Help me to know that my joy comes not from earthly matters or things, but is in You."

---

---

---

---

---

---

---

---

---

---

---

## Sixth Reflection

# Let your sins convict you, but not stop you, as you approach Our Lord

*Prayers: Our Father, Hail Mary, Glory be, Direct we beseech Thee, O Lord grant me... page 31.*

It is good if, when approaching Our Lord, your sins appear before you. But, these must not appear in order to condemn you, but to proclaim, since they are forgiven, God's mercy.[1] Let the memory of our sins humble us, and remind us of how we once freely pushed God away, and perhaps even allowed ourselves to remain in a life of sin, in a life where we treasured our sins. Thank the Lord for giving you an insight into the ugliness of sin, and ask Him to increase your hatred of sin, that you may always be pleasing to Him.

But, if these sins make you hesitate to approach Our Lord, heed the counsel of Saint Alphonsus:

> Say, then, to him often, O my Lord! wherefore dost Thou love me thus? What good thing dost Thou see in me? Hast Thou forgotten the injuries I have done Thee? But since Thou hast treated me so lovingly, and instead of casting me into hell, hast granted me so many favors, whom can I desire to love from this day forward but Thee, my God, my all? Ah, most gracious God, if in time past I have offended Thee, it is not so much the punishment I have deserved that now grieves me, as the

---

[1] This is why regularly going to Confession is so critical to a good spiritual life.

displeasure I have given Thee, who art worthy of infinite love. But Thou knowest not how to despise a heart that repents and humbles itself: *A contrite and humble heart, O God, Thou wilt not despise.*[2] Ah, now, indeed, neither in this life nor in the other do I desire any but Thee alone: *What have I in heaven? and besides Thee what do I desire upon earth! Thou art the God of my heart, and the God that is my portion forever.*[3] Thou alone art and shalt be forever the only Lord of my heart, of my will; Thou my only good, my heaven, my hope, my love, my all: "The God of my heart, and the God that is my portion forever."

The more to strengthen your confidence in God, often call to mind his loving treatment of you, and the gracious means he has used to drive you from the disorders of your life and your attachments to earth, in order to draw you to his holy love; and therefore fear to have too little confidence in treating with your God, now that you have a resolute will to love and to please him with all your power. The mercies he has granted you are most sure pledges of the love he bears you. God is displeased with a want of trust on the part of souls that heartily love him, and whom he loves. If, then, you desire to please his loving heart, converse with him from this day forward with the greatest confidence and tenderness you can possibly have.

One thing that may come to mind is the scene of Our Lord in the Garden of Gethsemane. He brings His Apostles,

---

[2] "Cor contritum et humiliatum, Deus, non despicies." Ps. 1. 19.

[3] "Quid enim mihi est in coelo? et a te quid volui super terram? . . . Deus cordis mei, et pars mea Deus in seternum." Ps. Ixxii. 25.

His closest friends, with Him into this moment of vulnerability and agony, where His fear is manifested, the fear He has toward the death He has chosen to endure for us. He eagerly asks them, "Could you not watch one hour with me?" The Church has always held out to us those words which came from His agonizing Heart. At the moment He said this to His Apostles, they did not fully understand what agonized Him; they did not fully understand the torture, torment, and death that He knew he was about to undergo. But, Our Lord knew, and this is what caused His agony. Notice, though, He did not run from this fate that He accepted from the Father – He embraced it, in order to liberate us from the reign of sin and the devil and to obtain, for us, healing and strength.

The Apostles, in their fatigue and ignorance and fear, were not able to console Our Lord, to pray with Him, to encourage Him. He was alone, except for the comfort He always had from the Father. As a man, he felt the absence of any true friend, of someone who could stand with Him, empathize, and suffer with Him. There was no one. His beloved friends fell asleep when He begged them to stay awake and pray with Him. He knew his betrayer was coming, and that this betrayer would set in motion His public rejection, humiliation, and death. Thus, He prayed and agonized.

Upon finding the Apostles sleeping, Our Lord rebuked them, but forgave them, understanding that they were exhausted and weak, and did not fully understand. We, however, know what Our Lord would later endure, and that He would rise from the dead and establish the Eternal Covenant and the path to salvation. Thus, for us, the request to spend time with Our Lord has a different quality and gravity. Remember what Saint Alphonsus said:

> The mercies he has granted you are most sure pledges of the love he bears you. God is displeased with a want of trust on the part of

souls that heartily love him, and whom he loves.

"The mercies" are clearly known to us, for He saved us from a life of darkness and sin by washing away our sins through Baptism and Confession, teaching us the Truth, and strengthening us with grace. Thus, we can merit eternal life through fidelity to Him.

*"Could you not watch one hour with me?"* Knowing what this means, what Our Lord went through for us, and how clearly we see that He loves us so much, it is no surprise that Saint Alphonsus states that Our Lord is "displeased" when we demonstrate a lack of trust in His love. Knowing what He embraced in order to demonstrate the intensity of His love, when one sacred sigh from His Heart could have redeemed us but, instead, He shed all of His blood, how is it that we still manifest a lack of trust in His love? But, is this not what the world and the devil want us to feel – apathy toward Our Lord? Indifference toward His suffering and death?

This effort of the fallen world and of the fallen angels, to move us toward apathy toward Our Lord, is what has encouraged us to sin. Renounce these sins! Renounce them out of love for Our Lord. It is also what has caused us to shy away from prayer, from trust in God's love, from confidence in speaking to Him. "You are sinful, and God prefers the pure," says the Devil, the Deceiver, "therefore, there is no point in approaching Him – He will not receive you." These lies of the fallen angels strike at the core of our spiritual focus – confidence in God.

Saint Therese, a Doctor of the Church, says it well:

> "Yes, I feel it; even though I had on my conscience all the sins that can be committed, I would go, my heart broken with sorrow, and throw myself into Jesus' arms, for I know how

much He loves the prodigal child who returns to Him."[4]

Therefore, let not even this most powerful weapon, your own sins and the shame you still feel, stop you from approaching Our Lord. Only, approach Him with sorrow for your sins, humility, and confidence in His love, and He will receive, forgive, and bless you. As you reflect on the image of Our Lord in agony in the Garden, remember that what He later endured on the Cross, was embraced in order to give you confidence to approach Him and ask for mercy!

~~~~~~~

## Considerations and Challenges

Find a good time where you are thinking clearly and are awake, and make a good examination of conscience. When you do, imagine you are in the presence of Our Lord in the Garden of Gethsemane. Name your sins and imagine they are in your hands: black, heavy, and repulsive. Name the sins that you may be aware of and planning to confess, and also name the sins that nag you and haunt you and which have left scars. Hold all these in your hands and extend them toward Our Lord. Listen to Our Lord praying in agony to the Father. Remember that the agony that He is embracing is both the consequence of, and the solution for, your spiritual and moral faults. Imagine Our Lord turning from His agony to acknowledge you, and what you hold in your hands. He says, calmly, "Your victory is in My passion. Leave here what you carry. Stay with Me. Pray." Remain there, as Our Lord returns to prayer with the Father. Observe His agony, which He endures to purify your heart. Pray, too, in reparation for

---

4 St. Thérèse. Story of a Soul: The Autobiography of St. Therese Of Lisieux. Washington: ICS Publications, 1975, page 259.

your sins, and for those who remain in their sins without a spirit of repentance.

Find a good, or at least a decent, Examination of Conscience. Avoid wasting time trying to find the "best" one. Set aside at least thirty minutes. Make an effort, perhaps heroic, to do this. Then, in prayer, in dialogue with Our Lord, through Our Lady's intercession, examine your conscience. The Holy Spirit will bring to light hidden sins and help you admit to these faults. Then, go to Confession at the next opportunity. Remember, one thorough effort at prayer, such as this, can initiate a complete change of approach to your spiritual life. God is living and active, and powerful, and desires your salvation. Give Him a moment, and He will offer you eternity.

Make a good examination of conscience when your mind is fresh. Get a guide, based on the Ten Commandments. Read and pray slowly through it. Don't think "I need to get through all 10," but focus on the Commandments one at a time, with the guiding questions. Focus. God will work in your conscience and bring to mind all of your sins, large and small, obvious and hidden, and give you clarity and sorrow for your sins and peace in longing for His mercy.

Talk to a good priest you may know. Ask him to guide you through a good Confession. Tell him what you are seeking: help in doing an examination of conscience and in making a deep Confession.

Set aside time to make one Holy Hour in Adoration. Offer this hour to Our Lord in reparation for all of your sins, for not staying with Him in those moments when you sinned. Prepare well, and do your best to be attentive for the entire hour. Know that Our Lord receives this hour from you and sees the love with which you offer it.

Consider writing down all of your sins on a piece of paper, in particular those sins with which you continue to struggle, or those sins which haunt you and your memories. Take the piece of paper and burn it. Before you burn it, look over the sins and say, out loud if possible, "In the Name of Jesus, I renounce (name the sin) and my attachment to it, and I accept Our Lord's mercy and healing graces."

## Seventh Reflection

# Approaching Our Lord with confidence, even when we are in desolation, inclined to complain, or burdened with our sins

*Prayers: Our Father, Hail Mary, Glory be, Direct we beseech Thee, O Lord grant me... page 31.*

Life brings crosses and miseries, misfortunes and inconveniences, sad and discouraging days, and burdens seemingly too heavy to bear. When we find ourselves in these situations, we are tempted to do one of two things: not speak to Our Lord about it, dealing with it all on our own strength and complaining to others about our burdens; or tell Him about it but feel like we are being ungrateful by complaining.

Saint Alphonsus counsels:

> Fear not that he will be offended if you sometimes gently complain, and say to him, *Why, O Lord, hast Thou retired afar off?*[1] Thou knowest, Lord, that I love Thee, and desire nothing but Thy love; in pity help me, and forsake me not. And when the desolation lasts long, and troubles you exceedingly, unite your voice to that of Jesus in agony and dying on the cross, and beseech his mercy, saying, *My God, my God, why hast Thou forsaken me?*[2] But let the effect of this be to humble you yet more

---

[1] "Ut quid, Domine, recessisti longe ?" Ps. ix. I.
[2] "Deus meus, ut quid dereliquisti me?" Matt, xxvii. 46.

at the thought that he deserves no consolations who has offended God; and yet more to enliven your confidence, knowing that God does all things, and permits all, for your good: *All things work together unto good.*[3] Say with great courage, even when you feel most troubled and disconsolate: *The Lord is my light and my salvation; whom shall I fear?*[4] Lord, it is Thine to enlighten me, it is Thine to save me; in Thee do I trust: *In Thee, O Lord, have I hoped; let me never be confounded.*[5]

Our Lord, in His agony on the Cross, cried out to the Father. In this great mystery, we are able to find comfort, when we, too, are permitted to suffer, and are inclined to cry out, "Where is the good God? Why must I suffer?" Remember, God did not create man to suffer, nor to die, but to live in peace with him on earth and in Heaven. It was sin that brought suffering and death. Sin is contrary to God's will. Thus, a world with suffering is part of the consequence of sin. Man, though, still desires and, almost instinctive to his nature, expects a life without suffering and death. We are inclined to peace and health and life. We cringe at suffering and death.

Nonetheless, we must accept suffering as permitted by God. Follow, as His trusting friend, the example of Our Lord and, when we offer our cry of agony to the Father, rest confident that He is there. Our Lord did not despair on the Cross, but spoke lovingly to the Father and continued to intercede for us. He embraced His death.

The effect of this cry to the Lord must be to humble us and enliven more confidence. For this to happen, the cry must be made with trust. If so, the cry will immediately remind you

---

[3] "Omnia cooperantur in bonum." Rom. viii. 28.
[4] "Dominus illuminatio mea et salus mea; quem timebo?" Ps. xxvi. i.
[5] "In te, Domine, speravi ; non confundar in aeternum." Ps. XXX. 2

that God is with you, and that all things work for good for those who love Him.

Perhaps it feels to you that the Lord is unduly silent, and has intentionally removed His presence from you, and silenced His voice. In these moments, remember that Our Lord is your Friend and Savior, but He is also your Master and Teacher. We must trust Him, learn from Him, and obey Him. We must be authentic as His disciples and friends. Let Him not be able to accuse us of a lack of faith! Just recall how He did so with the Apostles, and how ashamed they must have felt for not trusting their Lord. Yet, even then, He did not turn them away.

The Lord's silence is a way to teach us. Resist the temptation to think He has abandoned you, or that He is so displeased that He will not speak to you. Do not project onto Him the disorders that sinful creatures have! Our Lord is not spiteful, nor flighty, nor easily offended, nor quick-tempered, nor self-interested, nor emotional, nor does He hold grudges. Our Lord is patient, and kind, and slow to anger, and forgiving. He willingly suffers in His friendship with us, but only so that He may convert us.

Here we must pay attention to another very important area in our lives where our confidence and trust in Our Lord is often weak: the crippling power of guilt. When we sin, we face a far worse temptation to move away from the Lord than when our life is simply full of miseries or our prayer is empty and dry.

Saint Alphonsus has much wisdom to offer on this subject:

> Another mark of confidence highly pleasing to your most loving God is this: that when you have committed any fault, you be not ashamed to go at once to his feet and seek his pardon. Consider that God is so greatly inclined to pardon sinners that he laments their perdition, when they depart far from him and live as dead

to his grace. Therefore does he lovingly call them, saying, *Why will you die, O house of Israel? Return ye, and live.*[6] He promises to receive the soul that has forsaken him, so soon as she returns to his arms: *Turn ye to me, . . . and I will turn to you.*[7] Oh, if sinners did but know with what tender mercy the Lord stands waiting to forgive them! *The Lord waiteth, that He may have mercy on you.*[8] Oh, did they but know the desire he has, not to chastise, but to see them converted, that he may embrace them, that he may press them to his heart! He declares: *As I live, saith the Lord God, I desire not the death of the wicked, but that the wicked turn from his way and live.*[9] He even says: *And then come and accuse Me, saith the Lord: if your sins be as scarlet, they shall be made as white as snow.*[10] As though he had said, "Sinners, repent of having offended Me, and then come unto Me: if I do not pardon you, 'accuse Me;' upbraid Me, and treat Me as one unfaithful. But no, I will not be wanting to My promise. If you will come, know this: that though your consciences are dyed deep as crimson by your sins, I will make them by My grace as white as snow." In a word, he has declared that when a soul repents of having offended him, he forgets all its sins: *I will not remember all his iniquities.*[11]

As soon, then, as you fall into any fault, raise your eyes to God, make an act of love, and

---

[6] "Et quare moriemini, domus Israel? . . . Convertimini, et vivite. " Ezek. xviii. 31.

[7] "Convertimini ad me . . . et convertar ad vos." Zach. i. 3.

[8] "Expectat Dominus, ut misereatur vestri." Isa. xxx. 18.

[9] "Vivo ego, dicit Dominus Deus, nolo mortem impii, sed ut con- vertatur impius a via sua, et vivat." Ezek. xxxiii. n.

[10] "Et venite et arguite me, dicit Dominus; si fuerint peccata vestra ut coccinum, quasi nix dealbabuntur." Isa. 1, 18.

[11] "Omnium iniquitatum ejus . . . non recordabor." Ezek. xviii. 22.

with humble confession of your fault, hope assuredly for his pardon, and say to him, *Lord, behold he whom Thou lovest is sick;*[12] that heart which Thou dost love is sick, is full of sores: *heal my soul; for I have sinned against Thee.*[13] Thou seekest after penitent sinners; behold, here is one at Thy feet, who has come in search of Thee. The evil is done already; what have I now to do? Thou wilt not have me lose courage: after this my sin Thou dost still love me, and I too love Thee. Yes, my God, I love Thee with all my heart; I repent of the displeasure I have given Thee; I purpose never to do so any more. Thou, who art that God, *merciful and gracious, patient and of much compassion,*[14] forgive me; make me to hear what Thou didst say to the Magdalene, *Thy sins are forgiven thee;*[15] and give me strength to be faithful unto Thee for the time to come.

That thou mayest not lose courage at such a moment, cast a glance at Jesus on the cross; offer his merits to the Eternal Father; and thus hope certainly for pardon, *since he spared not even His own Son.*[16] Say to him with confidence, *Look on the face of Thy Christ.*[17] My God, behold Thy Son, dead for my sake; and for the love of that Son forgive me. Attend greatly, devout soul, to the instruction commonly given by masters of the spiritual life, after your unfaithful conduct, at once to have recourse to God, though you have repeated it a hundred times in a day; and after your falls, and the

---

[12] "Domine, ecce quern amas, infirmatur. John, xi. 3.
[13] "Sana animam meam, quia peccavi tibi." Ps. xl. 5.
[14] "Suavis et mitis, et multae misericordiae. " Ps. lxxxv. 5.
[15] "Remittuntur tibi peccata." Luke, vii. 48.
[16] "Proprio Filio suo non pepercit." Rom. viii. 32.
[17] "Respice in faciem Christi tui." Ps. lxxxiii. TO.

recourse you have had to the Lord (as has been just said), at once to be in peace. Otherwise, while you remain cast down and disturbed at the fault you have committed, your converse with God will be small; your trust in him will fail; your desire to love him grow cold; and you will be little able to go forward in the way of the Lord. On the other hand, by having immediate recourse to God to ask his forgiveness, and to promise him amendment, your very faults will serve to advance you further in the divine love. Between friends who sincerely love each other it often happens that when one has displeased the other, and then humbles himself and asks pardon, their friendship thereby becomes stronger than ever. Do you likewise; see to it that your very faults serve to bind you yet closer in love to your God.

God laments the perdition of sinners, crying out, *Why will you die, O house of Israel? Return ye, and live.*[18] Imagine Our Lord, looking across a city, arms outstretched, crying out these words, *Why will you die, O city of man? Return ye, and live!* He longs to press us to His Heart, but we so often refuse Him, not simply by our sins but by our self-misery afterward. We refuse to approach Him out of shame.

He swears to His mercy,[19] even giving us permission to accuse Him of infidelity if He does not pardon us. Saint Alphonsus says that we should call to mind the death of Lazarus, and remind Our Lord that the heart that He loves so much is ill and dying in sin, "Come, dear Lord, and raise it from the dead! The heart You love is sick! Remember You

---

[18] "Et quare moriemini, domus Israel? . . . Convertimini, et vivite. " Ezek. xviii. 31.

[19] Isaiah 1:18, as mentioned above in the quote from Saint Alphonsus

seek the penitent sinner – here is one! Remember You said not to lose courage – behold my need for You!"

Speak confidently to the Father, though always with great humility, presenting to Him the image of Christ crucified for our sake, for our forgiveness, for our reconciliation with the Father. It is when a soul is in sin that the Cross wields its power, not to destroy but to bestow life!

One power of sin is to destroy your confidence in God. Saint Alphonsus says to remember the advice of the masters of the spiritual life, that we should not wait one second to cast ourselves, with our sins, at the feet of the Lord, pleading for mercy. This shows humility, love, confidence, and friendship.

~~~~~~~

### Considerations and Challenges

Make a list of all the things that are burdensome, and about which you tend to complain. Then, pray to Our Lord, and hold out the list to Him, and say, "My Lord, I know that You do care about these concerns and complaints. You desire my peace and joy and stability. Please guide me, that I may not let these worries overpower me, nor lead me to take my eyes off of You. Stretch out Your hand to rescue me from the storm and waves, as you did to St. Peter. Let me not drown in this world of worries. My Jesus, I trust in You. Amen."

_____

_____

_____

_____

_____

_____

_____

_____

_____

_____

Go on a "date" with God: an outing, a hike, a picnic, to a café.
Have a conversation with Him, in this lively solitude, to talk
to Him, as a Friend, about your concerns, your goals, and
your worries.

Pick something in creation that you take for granted on a
daily basis, like birds, the sunrise, or the rain. Think about
how Our Lord cares for these creatures too. See how each
creature is capable of fulfilling the purpose it has been given
by God. Then read the Scripture verses below and reflect on
the fact that Our Lord cares so much more for you than He
does for these. Ask Him to grant you the grace to fulfill your
purpose, and to obey Him, and thus to be pleasing to Him.

"Therefore I tell you, do not be anxious about your life, what
you shall eat or what you shall drink, nor about your body,
what you shall put on. Is not life more than food, and the body
more than clothing? Look at the birds of the air: they neither
sow nor reap nor gather into barns, and yet your heavenly
Father feeds them. Are you not of more value than they? And
which of you by being anxious can add one cubit to his span
of life? And why are you anxious about clothing? Consider
the lilies of the field, how they grow; they neither toil nor
spin; yet I tell you, even Solomon in all his glory was not
arrayed like one of these. But if God so clothes the grass of
the field, which today is alive and tomorrow is thrown into
the oven, will he not much more clothe you, O men of little
faith? Therefore do not be anxious, saying, 'What shall we
eat?' or 'What shall we drink?' or 'What shall we wear?' For

the Gentiles seek all these things; and your heavenly Father knows that you need them all. But seek first his kingdom and his righteousness, and all these things shall be yours as well. Therefore do not be anxious about tomorrow, for tomorrow will be anxious for itself. Let the day's own trouble be sufficient for the day."[20]

[20] Matthew 6:25-34

# Eighth Reflection

## If the Father has given us even His own Son, He will not withhold from us any good

*Prayers: Our Father, Hail Mary, Glory be, Direct we beseech Thee, O Lord grant me... page 31.*

Saint Alphonsus calls us to remember always the fact that the Father has given us His own eternal Son.

In what ways has He given us the Son? He has given us His eternal Son, who is God himself, as a needy baby, dependent on us; as a family member, whose company we shared; as a boy, with whom we played and enjoyed our lives; as a wondrous gift, whom angels accompanied with messages of peace and hope; as an example of humility, simplicity, and obedience, who obeyed His parents in all things; as a man who loved the Father, that we may do the same; as a Teacher of all Truth, that we may leave the darkness of doubt, confusion, and lies; as the model of religion, that we may know how to worship God; as a hero, who opposed the enemies of mankind unto His own death on our behalf; as the God-man, who united us to God, both in His Incarnation and in His Rising from the dead; as the mighty God, Prince of Peace, Victor over Satan, Deliverer, Redeemer, and Messiah; as the God-man, our brother, our Friend, and our Eternal King. His whole mission and identity is tied to us.

In the light of that inexhaustive list of ways in which we are related to the Son of God, let us hear the words of Saint Alphonsus:

> Above all, animate your confidence at the thought of the gift that God has given us of

Jesus Christ: *God so loved the world as to give His only-begotten Son.*[1] How can we ever fear, exclaims the Apostle, that God would refuse us any good, after he has vouchsafed to give us his own Son? *He delivered Him up for us all; how hath He not also, with Him, given us all things?*[2]

*My delights are to be with the children of men.*[3] The paradise of God, so to speak, is the heart of man. Does God love you? Love him. His delights are to be with you; let yours be to be with himself, to pass all your lifetime with him, in the delight of whose company you hope to spend a blissful eternity. Accustom yourself to speak with him alone, familiarly, with confidence and love, as to the dearest friend you have, and who loves you best.

The Book of Proverbs, quoted above, speaks of the Wisdom of God, which the Church understands to be the Son of God. It teaches us that Our Lord, before His Incarnation, was with the Father in the creation of the world, and looked upon man with delight. It says that the Son was the delight of the Father, and that the Son now similarly delights in dwelling with man. What a tremendous joy this should bring! Oh, the sincerity of Our Lord's love for us! It is true and real, and we know this particularly through the event of the Incarnation, and beyond that, in the Passion and Death that He willingly embraced for us.

Take note of the times in Scripture where Our Lord demonstrates His delight to be with man, and to aid him. After being asked to heal the servant of a centurion, St. Luke, in his Gospel, simply states, *"and Jesus went with them."*[4] There is no hesitation, no second thought. The Lord goes to help

---

[1] "Sic enim Deus dilexit mundum, ut Filium suum unigenitum daret." John, iii. 16.
[2] "Pro nobis omnibus tradidit ilium; quomodo non etiam cum illo omnia nobis donavit?" Rom. viii.
[3] "Deliciae meae esse cum filiis hominum." Prov. viii. 31.
[4] Luke 7:6

him. When the Apostles were in fear of the storm and the angry sea while in a boat with Our Lord, they cried out to Him to help them, lest they drown.[5] Jesus awoke and immediately calmed the sea and the storm. He did not hesitate to act. He only rebuked them for their panic and lack of faith, as if He could not save them. When two blind men approached Him, He merely asked if they believed He could do this. When they said yes, He said, "*according to your faith be it done to you.*"[6] When a leper saw Jesus and fell on his face before Him, saying, "*Lord, if you will, you can make me clean,*" Our Lord immediately healed the man, saying, "*I will; be clean.*"[7] When two blind men approached Him in Jericho, crying out for mercy, Our Lord asked, "*What do you want me to do for you?' They said to him, "Lord, let our eyes be opened." And Jesus in pity touched their eyes, and immediately they received their sight and followed him.*"[8]

On at least two occasions, both tied to the suffering He would endure, Our Lord performs a miracle without anyone asking Him. In Naim, He raised from the dead the only son of a widow. At the end of the funeral procession, He took pity on the widow and, without being asked, raised the boy from the dead. He knew her pain, for His own Mother would soon feel a similar sorrow, and a similar joy upon His rising. *And when the Lord saw her, he had compassion on her and said to her, "Do not weep." And he came and touched the bier, and the bearers stood still. And he said, "Young man, I say to you, arise." And the dead man sat up, and began to speak. And he gave him to his mother.*[9] When He was being arrested, Our Lord healed the ear of one of the men who came to arrest Him, whom St. Peter had struck with a sword. This man was no friend of Our Lord, and did not even ask to be healed.[10] Healing the man right

---

[5] Luke 8:22ff
[6] Matthew 9: 27
[7] Luke 5:12-13
[8] Matthew 20: 32ff
[9] Luke 7:11ff
[10] Luke 22:51

then made it clear to all that Our Lord's mission was one of self-sacrifice and mercy, of pity and love for man.

Does Our Lord ever refuse one who asks for His help? No. However, He does require one thing of those he heals and aids – faith. On most occasions, Our Lord connects the healing or miracle He performed with the faith of the person, or the person's friends, who sought His assistance. A lack of faith is also shown to interfere with our union with the Lord, and His willingness to perform miracles. When He preached in the synagogue at Nazareth, *he did not do many mighty works there, because of their unbelief.*[11] When the Apostles attempted to cast out a demon and were unable, Our Lord revealed that it was their lack of faith which prevented them from doing it. He also adds that *this kind is not cast out but by prayer and fasting.*[12]

Any friendship requires trust in the other person. Even more so with Our Lord we must have trust. This trust, this faith, is the core of a strong friendship with the Lord. His is the supreme friendship. He is that Friend of all friends. So, when we are His friend, we must listen to Him, we must heed His word, we must long to be with Him, we must trust that He is always correct in His counsel, we must work to keep up this friendship above all other friendships.

And how, then, according to His own words, do we keep up this friendship? Prayer, fasting, taking up our cross, self-denial. To receive the good things of the Lord, we must stay united to Him. Friendship with Our Lord is discipleship.

Let us conclude this reflection with a powerful image that Our Lord gave us in the Gospel of John.[13] Read it now in the context of this reflection:

> "I am the true vine, and my Father is the vinedresser. [2] Every branch of mine that bears no fruit, he takes away, and every branch that

---

[11] Matthew 13:58
[12] Matthew 17:20 DR
[13] John 15:1-17

does bear fruit he prunes, that it may bear more fruit. ³ You are already made clean by the word which I have spoken to you. ⁴ Abide in me, and I in you. As the branch cannot bear fruit by itself, unless it abides in the vine, neither can you, unless you abide in me. ⁵ I am the vine, you are the branches. He who abides in me, and I in him, he it is that bears much fruit, for apart from me you can do nothing. ⁶ If a man does not abide in me, he is cast forth as a branch and withers; and the branches are gathered, thrown into the fire and burned. ⁷ If you abide in me, and my words abide in you, ask whatever you will, and it shall be done for you. ⁸ By this my Father is glorified, that you bear much fruit, and so prove to be my disciples. ⁹ As the Father has loved me, so have I loved you; abide in my love. ¹⁰ If you keep my commandments, you will abide in my love, just as I have kept my Father's commandments and abide in his love. ¹¹ These things I have spoken to you, that my joy may be in you, and that your joy may be full. ¹² "This is my commandment, that you love one another as I have loved you. ¹³ Greater love has no man than this, that a man lay down his life for his friends. ¹⁴ You are my friends if you do what I command you. ¹⁵ No longer do I call you servants, for the servant does not know what his master is doing; but I have called you friends, for all that I have heard from my Father I have made known to you. ¹⁶ You did not choose me, but I chose you and appointed you that you should go and bear fruit and that your fruit should abide; so that whatever you ask the Father in my name, he may give it to you. [17] This I command you, to love one another.

~~~~~~~

## Considerations and Challenges

Ask Our Lord to grant you the gift of true faith in Him.

Practice, for one whole day, seeing your day through the eyes of Our Lord. In this, see that He is the all-powerful One, and that all things are under His command. Thus, everything that happens in your day is willed by Him, either by His direct action or by His permission. Tell Him, at the beginning of that day, that you trust Him, and believe in Him as the Church teaches, and that you desire to let Him direct your entire day. Then, go about your day, and see that all that happens is under His Divine Providence. Let go of control over your day. Set aside your preferences regarding negotiable things. Slow down and let Him send things into your life. Receive all that happens, even sufferings, as things that He wills for you for that day. Remember Job.

Read the Book of Job.

Read the Book of Tobit.

Read Saint Alphonsus' *Uniformity With God's Will* (available online or through Catholic bookstores).

# Ninth Reflection

## To obtain the greatest goods, we must seek them, and actively speak to Our Lord, asking them of Him

*Prayers: Our Father, Hail Mary, Glory be, Direct we beseech Thee, O Lord grant me... page 31.*

Saint Alphonsus is quite clear, and it is logical to believe, that Our Lord waits for us to speak to Him before He showers us with His love. He is ever near to every one of us, but there are keys to "unlock His heart," so to speak. We must tell Him that we love Him, prove this in word and deed, repent of our sins, and remove worldly obstacles that stand in the way of His actions.

> "But seek first his kingdom and his righteousness, and all these things shall be yours as well."[1]

Our Lord wills that all men be saved, and He wills that all men love Him. As we know, this does not force us to do so – we must still choose Him, say "yes" to Him. This is His singular desire – that we say "yes" to Him. But, recall, that this is not in order to benefit Him, for He has no need of us. It is to benefit us. Our Lord does not need us, but we need Him. Our Lord created us to need Him. We are like plants, which need good soil, which need water, which need sun, which need attention and pruning. If all of these are provided, then we will produce great fruits.

---

[1] Matthew 6:33

Our Lord created us to need Him, as plants need earthly nourishment, and He has provided all of the spiritual sources of strength and nourishment that we could need.

Here, let us listen to the words of Saint Alphonsus:

> God will have himself esteemed the Lord of surpassing power and terribleness, when we despise his grace; but, on the contrary, he will have himself treated with as the most affectionate friend when we love him; and to this end he would have us often speak with him familiarly and without restraint.
>
> It is true that God ought always to be revered in the highest degree; but when he favors you by making you feel his presence and know his desire that you should speak to him as to that one who loves you above all, then express to him your feelings with freedom and confidence. *She preventeth them that covet her, so that she first showeth herself unto them.*[2] When you desire his love, he takes the first step, without waiting till you come to him; and presents himself to you, bringing with him the graces and the remedies you stand in need of. He only waits for you to speak to him, to show you that he is near to you, ready to hear and to comfort you: *And His ears are unto their prayers.*[3]
>
> By reason of his immensity, our God is in every place; but there are two places above all where he has his own peculiar dwelling. One is the highest heaven, where he is present by that glory which he communicates to the blessed; the other is upon earth, it is within the humble soul that loves him: *who dwelleth with a contrite*

---

[2] "Praeoccupat qui se concupiscunt, ut se illis prior ostendat." Wis. vi. 14.
[3] "Et aures ejus in preces eorum." Ps. xxxiii. 16

*and humble spirit.*[4] He, then, our God, dwelleth in the height of heaven; and yet he disdains not to occupy and engage himself day and night with his faithful servants in their cabins or their cells. And there he bestows on them his divine consolations, each one of which surpasses all the delights the world can give, and which he only does not desire who has no experience of them: *Oh, taste and see that the Lord is sweet.*[5]

Imagine a plant growing in a garden. The Gardener sees the plant and desires that it live, grow, and produce abundant fruit. So, the Gardener carefully clears away the weeds and grass that have begun to grow next to the plant, some of which have woven themselves around the plant itself. Carefully, the Gardener pulls against the base of the weeds, ripping them out from the root, and shaking them lightly to return the stolen soil to the plant. A few weeds are so close to the plant that the removal of them nearly uproots the plant as well. With all the weeds removed, the Gardener gently breaks up the soil around the plant, which had grown hard and dry from the many weeds and lack of rain. With the removal of all of the weeds complete, the soil and plant are now in great need of strength and nourishment, so the Gardener adds fresh, rich soil around the plant, and drenches the soil with fresh water. He repeats the process to ensure the soil is firm but not packed too tightly. When the ground is established, he then adds a layer of mulch to protect the plant from more weeds and from drying out too quickly should there be a lack of rain.

This is how Our Lord treats us, when we welcome Him to tend us with His love. He comes to us, as the Gardener to the plant, and we must simply say "yes" to His request. Then, through His sacraments, He purges, purifies, tills, plants,

---

[4] "In sancto habitans, et cum contrito et humili spiritu." Isa. lvii. 15
[5] "Gustate, et videte quoniam suavis est Dominus." Ps. xxxiii. 9.

feeds, and protects our souls. He calls us to His love through His sacraments, which are powerful. When we have recourse to them, and work with Our Lord to keep the weeds out and the soil rich, the sacraments lead to the product of great spiritual fruits and strength. It is through them that Our Lord removes the weeds, that Our Lord replenishes the soil, that Our Lord protects the graces that have been imparted, and that Our Lord causes fruits to be produced through our faith in Him.

See, then, yourself as this plant, this flower, planted by Our Lord. Admit to Him that you have grown weak, or have been weak in the past, and have weeds and dry and weak soil. Give Him permission to tear into the weeds and dirt, to infuse new life into your soul, and to allow you to grow and bear fruit.

Speak to Him sincerely and constantly. While rote, memorized, prayers are good, they are not enough. Speak directly to Him, as His child and as His friend. Tell Him to give you courage and confidence, if that is what you lack. Ask Him to give you humility if that is what you need. But, speak to Him directly, and sincerely, and from the heart, and from your faith. Be honest. Do you struggle with truly believing? Tell Him. He will aid your faith. "I believe; help my unbelief!"[6]

Do you look at Our Lord in a way that Saint Alphonsus describes, or do you see Him as remote and far off, or angry and cruel, or disinterested and concerned only about things much bigger than your tiny life? Tell Our Lord this. Ask Him to remove the shroud, the blanket of lies that covers your mind from seeing Him as this wonderful God who loves. Tell Him that you have believed the lies that God is cruel, far off, unconcerned, and so strict that none can be pleasing to Him.

Tell Him you need Him to shatter the defenses you have established that prevent you from trusting Him. Tell Him that you long for the freedom that the great Saints had – the freedom of the ones who know they are loved by the all-

---

[6] Mark 9:24

powerful God, the all-powerful God who loves man so much that He Himself became man.

~~~~~~~

## Considerations and Challenges

Find an image of the Most Sacred Heart of Jesus. Look at His Heart, and focus on the details you see in this image. Then look into His eyes. Let Him look into your eyes, through this sacred icon. Do not look upon this image as a painting, but as Our Lord Himself.

Re-read the quote, "I believe; help my unbelief," in context: Mark 9:20-26. Reflect on the reaction of Our Lord when the father of the boy does not express confidence in Our Lord's ability. Note, then, what Our Lord says is truly necessary.

> And they brought the boy to him; and when the spirit saw him, immediately it convulsed the boy, and he fell on the ground and rolled about, foaming at the mouth. And Jesus asked his father, "How long has he had this?" And he said, "From childhood. And it has often cast him into the fire and into the water, to destroy him; but if you can do anything, have pity on us and help us." And Jesus said to him, "If you can! All things are possible to him who believes." Immediately the father of the child cried out and said, "I believe; help my unbelief!" And when Jesus saw that a crowd came running together, he rebuked the unclean spirit, saying to it, "You dumb and deaf spirit, I command you, come out of him, and never enter him again." And after crying out and convulsing him terribly, it came out.

# Conclusion

As this may be the end of your Retreat, look back over all of your notes. Read them in order, all in one sitting. Make a note of any themes that emerged. Then, write down the most important items in the lines below. Finally, take these essential ideas, and compose a prayer to Our Lord which addresses these to Him. Say this prayer every day, for as long as it continues to bear fruit.

If you benefitted from the writings of Saint Alphonsus, consider reading more from this Doctor of the Church. Also, consider taking him as one of your patron Saints, to whom you turn, in particular, for assistance in living out the Christian life. Often, our patron Saints choose us, or God directly sends them into our lives. Either way, he, and all of the Saints mentioned in this book, love you with the love of Christ, and are present with you to guide you safely to Our Lord, in this present moment and into eternity.

# About the Author

Charles D. Fraune is the founding Theology teacher of Christ the King Catholic High School in Huntersville, NC and was a Theology teacher there for ten years. He left teaching on the high school level to found the *Slaying Dragons Apostolate* and *Slaying Dragons Press*, as a result of the response to his best-selling spiritual warfare book, <u>Slaying Dragons: What Exorcists See & What We Should Know</u>. This Apostolate is dedicated to sharing the wisdom of spiritual warfare from the counsel of modern public exorcists in the context of the Church's two-thousand-year history of authoritative teaching on the subject.

In addition to the above, he has taught nearly every grade level, from second grade to adult, including on the college and diocesan level. He spent three semesters in seminary with the Diocese of Raleigh at St. Charles Borromeo Seminary in Pennsylvania. This completed a nine-year discernment of the priesthood and religious life after which he discerned that Our Lord was not calling him to the priesthood. He has a Master of Arts in Theology from the Christendom College Graduate School, as well as an Advanced Apostolic Catechetical Diploma. His enjoyment of writing began over twenty years ago and culminated in his first completed book, <u>Come Away By Yourselves</u>, a guide to prayer for busy Catholics. He has also written a spiritual warfare manual for youth and their parents, called <u>Swords and Shadows: Navigating Youth Amidst the Wiles of Satan</u>, and a companion book to <u>Slaying Dragons</u>, which serves as a workbook, study guide, and spiritual warfare manual, called <u>Slaying Dragons – Prepare for Battle: Applying the Wisdom of Exorcists to Your Spiritual Warfare.</u>

Find him at: **SlayingDragonsPress.com**

# Slaying Dragons Press

*Slaying Dragons Press,* founded in 2021, is the fruit of a spiritual work begun in 2016 which sought to find new ways to bring people the joy and beauty of the Catholic Faith. By God's Providence, what began under the name *The Retreat Box* has grown into *The Slaying Dragons Apostolate* and *Slaying Dragons Press.*

This work is a grassroots apostolate which thrives on support and endorsements from those who enjoy these books. As a result, fans of the books and supporters of the mission help increase the reach of *Slaying Dragons Press* by telling friends, family, priests, religious, and Bishops about these books.

Please consider supporting this work in any way that you can. While *Slaying Dragons Press* is *not* a non-profit, financial support is always welcome. Please visit SlayingDragonsPress.com for ways to support this apostolate. If you do not have a copy of the other celebrated books we have published, get one today!

*Support this work on **Patreon**
~patreon.com/**theslayingdragonsapostolate**

***Subscribe to the author's website for discounts and news**
~SlayingDragonsPress.com/pages/**Subscribe**

# Popular Slaying Dragons Press Titles

*The Occult Among Us: Exorcists and Former Occultists Expose the Nature of This Modern Evil*

*The Rise of the Occult: What Exorcists & Former Occultists Want You to Know*

*Slaying Dragons: What Exorcists See & What We Should Know* (also in Spanish – *Matando Dragones*)

*Slaying Dragons - Prepare for Battle: Applying the Wisdom of Exorcists to Your Spiritual Warfare*

*Swords and Shadows: Navigating Youth Amidst the Wiles of Satan*

*Come Away By Yourselves: A Guide to Prayer for Busy Catholics*

# Slaying Dragons Press

www.ingramcontent.com/pod-product-compliance
Lightning Source LLC
Chambersburg PA
CBHW021646120626
46545CB00002B/730